THE JOY OF SPIRITUAL GROWTH

THE JOY OF
Spiritual
Growth

REAL ENCOUNTERS

∎ ∎ ∎

Frank Rose and Robert Maginel

SWEDENBORG FOUNDATION PUBLISHERS
WEST CHESTER, PENNSYLVANIA

Inquiries about the program described in this book may be directed to:
The Arizona Spiritual Growth Foundation, Inc.
8421 E. Wrightstown Road
Tucson, Arizona 85715

Library of Congress Cataloging-in-Publication Data
Rose, Frank, 1927–
     The joy of spiritual growth : real encounters / Frank Rose and
Robert Maginel.
          p.   cm.
     Includes bibliographical references (p.   ).
     ISBN 0-87785-384-3
     1. Spiritual life—Christianity.   2. Emotions—Religious aspects–
–Christianity.   3. Conduct of life.   I. Maginel, Robert.
II. Title.
BV4501.2.R667   1999
248.4'894—dc21   99-34380
                                                                         CIP

Credits: Art on p. 161 by Owen Rose; translation of all Bible passages
and Lord's Prayer (p. 167) by Jonathan Rose
Edited by Betty Christiansen
Cover designed by Helene Krasney
Interior design by Gopa Design & Illustration
Set in Berkeley by Matrix, York, Pennsylvania

Printed in the United States of America

For more information, contact:
Swedenborg Foundation Publishers
320 North Church Street
West Chester, PA 19380
(610) 430-3222
or
http://www.swedenborg.com.

CONTENTS

INTRODUCTION

W̳E OFTEN THINK OF LIFE as a journey from one location to another. Our destination on this journey is usually a goal: earning a degree, getting married, or obtaining a promotion, for example. Our lives are goal-oriented, and we spend much of our time and energy moving toward those goals.

Yet the road to achieving any goal may not be as straightforward as we planned. We may intend to obtain a college degree and then proceed to a high-paying, prestigious job. But, along the way, we encounter either obstacles or interruptions that cause us to veer off course. Perhaps at some point during our college years, we fall in love, get married, and start a family. This may lead more directly to the job market than was anticipated and to the kind of job that was not originally envisioned. Still, it is always possible to get back to the original goal..

Life is full of similar pursuits of material goals. However, we can lose sight of another and more important dimension to our lives as we concentrate on reaching our desired destinations. The dimension of our lives that we often ignore is the spiritual dimension where we deal with the important issues such as our core values, our dealings with other people, and our inner feelings about ourselves. In this dimension, we also work on our relationship with the higher power in our lives. These are the issues that will transcend our death.

Spiritual growth is about recognizing this special dimension of our lives and nurturing it to attain peace and satisfaction. This growth is about attaining something that cannot be achieved through goals that relate to the external and material aspects of our lives. In spiritual growth, we concentrate our attention on those dimensions of our lives that have an impact on every moment we live. We also believe that this dimension is the only reality of our life hereafter.

Throughout our lives we are growing. Our bodies reach a peak of physical perfection somewhere in our twenties, but the spirit continues to develop throughout life. Normally, we begin to learn even before birth and go on learning up to the moment of death. We not only learn, but we also grow internally in many ways.

This is spiritual growth, but it does not always proceed in an upward curve. Many times we may feel as if our lives are going downhill, and we are losing our ability to cope. What can we do to cooperate with our spiritual growth and help it to go in a positive direction?

We can see many parallels between physical and spiritual growth. The human body develops at its own rate. We really do not have to work to make it grow. Even so, there are many ways that we can promote or interfere with that growth. Exercise and nutrition are important factors in our physical growth.

There are also many ways that we can strengthen our spiritual well-being. We can do this through prayer, meditation, and the reading of the Bible and other religious literature. We can do it through participating in rituals, nurturing family and friends, and strengthening family relationships. We benefit our spiritual lives through taking responsibility for being useful in society. These aspects of our spiritual life are analogous to exercise and nutrition in our physical lives.

We are all progressing spiritually as we go through life, and this growth will take place despite what we do. So why should we be interested in working on our spiritual growth?

To understand this inner process of spiritual growth, we must picture ourselves as under two sets of influences, one negative and one positive. We must also understand that these forces naturally invade our consciousness and must avoid the mistake of thinking that we are somehow inherently negative. We come to learn that we are just human individuals who are subject to both good and bad pressures in our lives. The spiritual growth program described in this book provides many methods for recognizing and dealing with the negative pressures that come up in daily living.

Essentially, spiritual growth is a positive process, but that process is seriously impaired by thoughts and feelings that drag us down. In addition to doing the positive things that support the spiritual side of our life, we need to learn how to deal with the negative. This requires tools, and using new tools requires work.

Suppose you wanted to improve your health by going to weekly lectures on the basics of diet and exercise but never actually did the exercise or changed your diet accordingly. In a similar manner, we need to learn about our own spirituality, and we need to participate in developing it. We have long wondered about spiritual growth, how it is achieved, and what can be done to foster it.

A Canadian friend who is a keen gardener shared about his search "for the happy radish." He had grown many radishes in his life, and every season would look again at the conditions that the radishes seemed to enjoy best. "A happy radish is a growing radish," he would say, "but what makes a radish happy?" He knew that he could create soil conditions. He had some control over the amount of shade (and so, indirectly, over the amount of sunlight) in his radish patch. He could remove weeds. But he could not make the radishes grow. All he could do was to provide conditions in which the radishes would be content enough to grow.

Isn't this also true of spiritual life? Growth is part of life, and life flows into all of us from God. We cannot make ourselves grow. We can enrich the soil of our minds by study. We can bask in the warmth of a supportive group of people, and we can take steps to remove the weeds and other barriers to growth. We can provide the conditions for spiritual growth.

Before going further, we need to look at the fact that sometimes it is useless to do spiritual work until an external situation is changed. This is "the-pebble-in-the-shoe situation."

Suppose you're walking along, and you get a pebble in your shoe. It may seem so small that you ask yourself, "Is it worth stopping and taking off the shoe?" But suppose a man has a pebble in his shoe over a long period. He ignores it and the fact that it makes him limp slightly. Then, his back starts to go out, which, in turn, leads to headaches and feelings of depression. At this point, the man might go to the psychiatrist for depression, to a doctor for the backache. He might get some pills and advice to relieve his conditions, but the problems keep coming back because he has never removed that pebble in his shoe.

Sometimes you need to remove the pebble, the root cause of the problem, before you can deal with the headache or the backache. Sometimes you need to make a change in your life before you can do spiritual work. For example, a person in an abusive relationship might go for help in trying to deal with anger and fear. So long as the abuse continues, there is very little point in working on those feelings. It might be necessary for the person to get out of the destructive relationship first, and *then* work on the residual effects of anger, frustration, and guilt. Another example is a person who is actively involved in substance abuse. So long as he or she continues to indulge in this behavior, it is virtually impossible to do any spiritual work about it. Before coming to a spiritual-growth group, an addictive person needs to deal with the addiction and, having dealt with the root cause, can then work on other issues in his or her spiritual life. Of course, it is not always as simple as that, but the general rule still stands: people need to have some kind of order and peace in their lives before working on spiritual issues.

The growth envisioned in this program moves the participants from the pain of negativity to the pleasure of peace of mind. It is also designed to increase self-awareness and improve comfort with the participant's humanity. In its simplest sense, the program is designed to move the participant from the depths of negative emotions to the sunshine of higher delights in life. Anyone who has been successful with this program has enjoyed an improved outlook on his or her personal existence. The objective of this program is to gain an ongoing and closer relationship with your God by removing those obstacles that block out the flow of love into your life.

THE BACKGROUND OF THE
ARIZONA SPIRITUAL GROWTH MOVEMENT

In 1988, a group of twelve people in the Sunrise Chapel congregation in Tucson, Arizona, met to discuss the possibility of setting up some kind of program for spiritual growth. In the end, we decided to center weekly meetings around a series of tasks.

We settled on the twelve tasks that form the chapters of this book, although the group met for thirteen weeks, which provided an opportunity to report on the twelfth task. We presented the course to several groups, produced a manual that other groups could follow, and mailed them to people in various parts of the world.

The sessions proved to be very enjoyable. We found that it was fun to work on our spiritual life. This is something that we could enjoy as individuals and also enjoy as a group. We laughed at our human foibles and shared the struggle of keeping ourselves working on living a spiritual life. The sessions provided a safe place to for each participant to be him- or herself, without risk of judgment.

People often commented that they felt much better at the end of the sessions than when they arrived. It was wonderful to discover practical ways of gaining more peace of mind and spiritual balance. It was fun to do so with other people who were doing the same. In these groups, people were accepted as they were and applied what was discussed directly to their immediate lives.

From these initial efforts, a pattern of lectures, meditations, and tasks evolved. This pattern was based on three generic tasks:

1. Improving one's relationship with self
2. Improving one's relationships with others
3. Improving one's relationship with a higher power.

Literally hundreds of individual tasks have been developed in working through these generic categories. Specific tasks range from exercises that encourage the participant to "live in the

xii INTRODUCTION

present moment" to tasks that aid the individual in "turning his or her life over to the Lord." Each task is structured and interpreted by the individual participant so that he or she may find application in his or her own life.

The sessions transcribed in this book are taken from workshops that began in September1998 and ended in December 1998. The transcripts have, of course, been edited, so that irrelevant material was excluded, although no one's words or reactions were altered in any way. There were fourteen participants, from a wide variety of religious and professional backgrounds. Although the names used are pseudonyms, the people you come to meet are real. You can read biographical information in "The Group," on pages 169–170.

There are many positive ways to work on your spiritual life. These include praying, meditating, worshiping, being useful, and doing many other constructive things that can range from personal development to community service. But always remember: no matter how good and powerful these positive steps may be, they are easily undermined by negativism.

Jesus summarized this positive attitude in the two great commandments that we find in Matthew 22:37–40: "You shall love the Lord your God with all your heart and with all your soul and with all your mind" and "You shall love your neighbor as yourself." Yet there remains the question about how we come to love the Lord and our neighbor. This book is based on the assumption that one of the first steps is to remove those negative things in us that block the flow of our love to God and to each other. We can remove the blocks through a series of spiritual growth tasks explained in this book.

HOW TO USE THIS BOOK

As was mentioned, this book describes the kind of work that is done in a spiritual-growth workshop and includes transcripts from actual sessions. As you read, you might want to imagine yourself as part of the group, learning about the tasks, doing them, and even recording them in a spiritual journal, as the actual participants are encouraged to do.

As part of the course, the group leaders hand out sheets that specify enrichment reading from three main sources: the Bible, the theological works of Emanuel Swedenborg, and the work *Psychological Commentaries on the Works of Gurdjieff and Ouspensky* by Maurice Nicoll. Other resources are recommended as well.

The participants are invited to keep a spiritual journal so that they can observe their progress over the twelve-week period. They are also encouraged to share whatever "gems of wisdom" they might have thought of, read, or been told since the last session.

The sessions last approximately ninety minutes and follow a general outline:

- Introduction, with each person responding to the question "How are you?"
- Meditation
- "Gems of wisdom" shared by each participant
- Reports on each participant's experience of the assigned task
- Discussion about new task (a three-to-five minute presentation that can be based on a chapter in this book)
- Closing thoughts from each participant
- Closing prayer. Each group may choose its own method of closure.

In seminars sponsored by the Arizona Spiritual Growth Foundation, we often use a special rendition of The Lord's Prayer, translated by Jonathan Rose, which appears on page 167 of this book. This translation offers a new experience for those who are used to a rote recital of the traditional prayer, one that makes them think about what the words could mean to them. It also gives the group something to share that is unique and offers a means of identifying with the program. However, at other times, we have listened to recorded music or have had a moment of silent prayer.

The following guidelines will prove helpful in forming a group and in working together:

- Use local newspapers and other media to announce a free course to attract participants seeking spiritual awareness.
- Ask each participant to commit to the full twelve-week series.
- Charge each participant only for the cost of materials, such as books purchased or photocopied materials. The underlying principle of the course is that spiritual growth is freely given and so should be shared freely.
- Designate one person to act as group leader; this person must understand that his or her main function is to make sure that the guidelines are followed, not to act as an expert or to give advice. Depending upon the group composition and "personality," it also works well if the participants take turns with the leadership role.
- Get the group to follow certain rules. The spiritual growth guidelines that have worked best in the many sessions we have led are the following:

1. We do not give advice.
2. We do not interrupt.
3. We speak only for ourselves.
4. We share; we don't preach.
5. We have the option to pass.
6. We understand that there are no failures, only opportunities.
7. We do not identify individuals when sharing our experiences.
8. We keep confidential all experiences that are shared within the group.
9. We start and end all meetings promptly.
10. We do not smoke, eat, or drink during meetings.

This book can be used profitably either by an individual reader or by a group acting toward a common end. It can also be used by couples as a way of working on their spiritual lives together. This, in turn, will benefit their relationship. No matter how or by whom the program is used, it is designed to help people reach a higher level of spiritual awareness and inner peace and to enjoy the great rewards of spiritual growth.

THE JOY OF SPIRITUAL GROWTH

TASK 1

Waking Up to Spiritual Life

Keep awake, therefore, because you don't know what day your master is coming. Surely you recognize that if the homeowner had known during which night-watch the thief was coming, he would have stayed awake and would not have allowed his house to be invaded.

Matthew 24:42, 43

People who have not been reborn are like those who are dreaming. People who have been reborn are like those who are awake. In fact, in the Word, natural life is compared to being asleep and spiritual life to being awake.

Emanuel Swedenborg, *True Christian Religion* 606

Natural life in and of itself, apart from spiritual life, is nothing but being asleep. But having a natural life with a spiritual life inside it is being awake.

Emanuel Swedenborg, *Apocalypse Revealed* 158

GROWTH IS LIFE, and life is growth. Parents of a newborn continually watch for signs of development in their child, and they rejoice at each new phase. If the baby seemed to make no progress at all, they would be extremely alarmed.

We take this physical growth for granted, but what of spiritual growth? Just like a parent of a small child, a person who feels stuck spiritually can become very distressed when it seems he or she is not making any progress. In that distress, a question is likely to arise: "What can I do to advance my spiritual journey?"

We may ponder whether our spiritual life progresses without any thought on our part, as our physical development does. When we grow restless with the situation we are in or feel "stuck" spiritually, we look for some way to cooperate with our own spiritual growth, even if we do not have a very clear idea of what that means or what it involves.

THE HOUSE

Imagine yourself in a house that has no lights or windows. Imagine that you are exploring it with only a small flashlight. You would only be conscious of the part of the house that came within the beam of your small light.

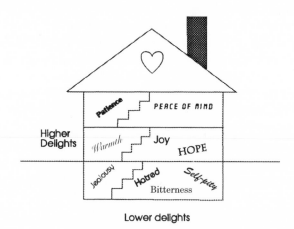

Our consciousness is like that narrow beam in the house that is our total being. Most people are conscious of only a very small part of their total being. They are like people who live in a mansion, but think that the house consists only of a small apartment below ground level. They might not like this apartment much. It is dark and damp, full of spiders, roaches, and other little beasts.

They may attempt to clean up the apartment, but no improvement seems to last very long. The spiders and roaches keep coming back, no matter how many they kill. They end up living, as Thoreau said, "lives of quiet desperation."

Any attempt to remodel this apartment has very limited results, and some problems are so deep, they are beyond any attempt to solve them. But through spiritual growth, we get to look at the quality of this basement apartment in ourselves, and we observe it for what it is. This involves telling ourselves the truth about the kind of thoughts and feelings that occupy much of our conscious life. If that little apartment was all we had to our house—if our negative thoughts and feelings were all there was to us—this could be extremely depressing. Much like the spiders and roaches in that apartment, negative thoughts and emotions are "beasts" that thrive in the basements of our minds.

Spiritual growth begins by discovering that we have higher levels in ourselves. Our mansions include much more than this dank little basement room. When we learn how to access higher levels of the mansion, we find that they are of a very different quality. They are light and cheerful. They have windows you can see out, so you can enjoy the beautiful world outside. These higher levels are free of all those little beasts that make such a noise and smell in the basement.

For the most part, negative emotions such as fear, jealousy, self-pity, and shame are in the lowest levels of the house. When one of these emotions is active, it feels as if our whole life centers in the basement, but the reality is that the higher levels of our mind are calm and peaceful.

How do we access these higher levels of our house? We cannot raise ourselves by our own bootstraps, so to speak. The basement cannot rise and become the first or second floor of our house. Instead, we can use techniques to shift our sense of who we are to a different level of our life. For example, if we are overwhelmed by feelings of fear, our lives seem to be nothing but fear. Fear seems to be who we really are. Yet at other moments when our fear is gone, we can hardly remember it.

We normally think of ourselves as one person who has certain qualities and characteristics. A person might say: "Well, I am a worrier. My mother was a worrier; it runs in the family, so I guess I will always be a worrier. I can't do much about it."

The error lies in thinking that we are just one person with certain distinct qualities, when, in fact, we are many different people with many different qualities. One of our personalities is lazy and uncaring. Another is committed and deeply interested in other people. One part of us is quietly reflective, yet another is active and boisterous. Parts of us are mean, deceitful, and self-serving. Other parts are generous, truthful, and interested in being useful to others. Rather than rejecting ourselves for being mean, we can simply observe that undesirable part and simultaneously get in touch with the parts that are more giving.

Our house consists of many levels. The basement level is full of "beasts," meaning our negative emotions. The stairs show us that we can access higher levels, though in reality, we do not so much ascend the stairs as we shift our sense of who we are from the basement to some other level.

We don't exactly get out of the basement; the basement is always there. Rather, the light in the basement goes off, and our attention shifts to the light in the higher stories. We no longer sense that *we are* the basement.

Another aspect of the basement is that we cannot see out the basement windows. This suggests that while we identify ourselves with our lower selves, we also cannot really see other people. We are too wrapped up in ourselves.

The diagram shows a heart in the attic, to represent that at the highest level of our being, we are perfect vessels of the pure love of God. That is where the divine life flows into us most directly and is received in the best way. In our organized spiritual-growth group, we use a meditation that says: "I know that I am a spiritual being, created in the image and likeness of God. On the deepest level, I am at peace and in harmony with the universe. I am a beloved child of God, a vessel. The Lord works through me as his instrument. I find my greatest fulfillment when his love passes through me to others who are also his children, who are also created in his image and likeness." The final chapter of this book contains a sample meditation.

You are the only one who can access your own higher levels. You alone live in your inner world. This is why we ask you to test everything in this book against your own experience. In the end, you will not learn from this book, but from what you have experienced while working through it.

Some people like to record their spiritual experiences in a journal, as this helps them to be aware of exactly when they do a spiritual task and what happens as a result. Keeping a spiritual journal is another way of staying awake. It can help you to be more conscious of your spiritual life and how your spiritual growth is evolving.

The mind is the inner world of thoughts and feelings, imagination, desire, reason, intuition, and so on. These span a vast range of qualities, from the sublime to the ridiculous. We call some feelings negative: emotions such as self-pity, contempt, smugness, impatience, fear, and anger. Other emotions are more positive, such as compassion, joy, happiness, tenderness, and excitement. There are some emotions that run so deep that they lie almost beyond consciousness: feelings of profound inner peace, contentment, trust, and bliss.

This suggests that there are different levels of emotions and thoughts. Some are very crude and negative. These emotions live in the damp and dingy basement of the mansion that we call the human mind. People even talk of themselves as "down in the dumps" when they are in unpleasant moods. At other times, they say they are "on cloud nine" or "on a spiritual high."

To make this journey from the lower to the higher levels of the mind, we need to realize that there is a need for growth. It also helps to have an idea of what our present life is like, plus an idea of how to move to a better life.

FINDING YOUR STARTING POINT

Suppose you are waiting for someone coming to visit you. This person is late. The phone rings, and you hear your friend's voice on the phone, saying, "I am lost!" What do you say?

"Where are you?" you might ask. Your visitor might then say, "I told you, I am lost." You might reply, "Well, where are you phoning from?" If the person answers, "I don't know," you might then ask for some identifying landmark, such as a crossroad, a building with a name on it, or anything else in their environment.

Once you are given this information, it is unlikely that you would then reply, "Sorry, you are in the wrong place," and then hang up.

Wherever your visitor is is the *right place*, because that is where he or she is. You need to know where that place is if you are to help that person find a new place. The same is true spiritually. Your spiritual journey begins by locating where you are with your emotions and thoughts. This requires self-observation, and it must be done accurately and lovingly.

If you arrived at the scene of an accident and saw bodies strewn along the road, you might call for a doctor. Suppose the doctor came, looked at the scene, and said, "Oh this is terrible, it is just awful. I can't stand the sight of all that blood. My stomach turns when I see all that damage." You would call for a different doctor. What is needed is a clinical analysis of the reality of the situation, not an emotional or judgmental response.

The same is true of our response to ourselves when we take what has been called a "moral inventory." We must observe. We must first notice what is there, and then we can see what needs to be done to make things better. Then, we will begin moving to a better place.

Before our journey begins, it is as if we are fast asleep. We may be very much aware of the world around us, and we may be very successful in business or in acquiring possessions. Still, our inner world might be in constant turmoil and pain.

How different it would be to think that life is miserable not because of external circumstances, but because we are living in the gloomiest part of our mind. We do not need new possessions or new relationships to enjoy life more, we simply need to make an inner journey.

The journey begins with a wake-up call. For some people, this happens in connection with some crisis in their lives. Their spouse leaves them. They find themselves lying drunk in a gutter. They can't put down that drink or needle. They feel suicidal and alone.

Some people are deeply grateful for bottoming out in that way, not because it is a pleasant experience, but because the trauma of the experience opens up an entirely new and different phase of their life. They begin to wake up.

BEING ASLEEP

In Matthew 26:41, we read, "Stay awake and keep praying so that you won't come into a crisis. The spirit is eager, but the flesh is sick."

"Stay awake" means "wake up." Our first task in a program of spiritual growth is to wake up to spiritual life. Think of how many crimes are committed by people who are spiritually asleep. All negativity comes because we are asleep to the spiritual aspect of our lives.

Once, while a man was sleeping in his bed, a robber broke down his front door, walked into his house, and robbed him of his possessions. Just before leaving, the robber started beating the man with a baseball bat. The man woke up to a barrage of blows and soon was beaten unconscious. His first thought when he came to was, "If only I had been awake, I could have done something to stop myself from being robbed and beaten."

This is a parable of our spiritual life. Our negative emotions are like the thief. They invade our thoughts, rob us of peace of mind, destroy our relationships, and spiritually beat us up. Let's take an example.

A man returns from work, tired and frustrated, to find the house is littered with toys. He marches off to find his child happily playing in his room, and begins to shout at him. In no time, the child is crying and the man's wife appears, angry at him for scolding so harshly. Soon the entire family is upset, and the man mutters to himself, "I don't know what came over me! How did that happen?"

On a spiritual level, it is as if anger came sneaking into his heart, closely followed by frustration, self-pity, fear, and a host of other negative feelings. They took over his mind and body, and he found himself yelling at the child he loves, fighting with his wife, and upsetting the entire family, all because he was spiritually asleep! If he were spiritually awake, would he fly into a rage like that over nothing? Being asleep, he was robbed of his love, his peace of mind, his sanity, and possibly his family's trust.

Does a father start the day saying to himself, "Today I would like to do untold emotional damage to my daughter by calling her stupid and ugly"? If he looked on it as a choice, he would never choose to do anything that would harm his child. Instead, because of his lack of awareness, he falls into patterns of criticism and put-downs that slowly damage his daughter emotionally. In a more conscious state, he wouldn't do that.

Does a woman start the day with the resolve to make her children and her husband's lives miserable by reprimanding them until they want to leave home? Does a child make a conscious decision to annoy and pester the people around her until they want to wring her neck?

Why do people do these negative things? Would they do them if they were spiritually awake? Think how vital it is, then, to be spiritually conscious.

Not everyone has such a dramatic reminder of the need for growth. Some people just find that life has very little meaning, or they find themselves chronically unhappy or frustrated. A young woman once told her pastor, "I am a successful woman. I have a good job, a nice home. I am married with three children. I go to church every Sunday. I participate in the youth group. I help on church committees, and I do everything that I thought would make me happy. Yet I am miserable. What's wrong?" The minister replied, "It looks as if it is time to begin the inward journey."

The next question is, "How do I do that?"

You may have had the experience of being in a vivid dream. The dream seems so real that you do not know whether you are asleep or awake. Perhaps you remember to pinch yourself. That is a way of waking up.

DIVIDING YOUR ATTENTION

Waking up requires effort, and there are many ways it can be done. One way is called dividing your attention.

In this method, we take advantage of the fact that we are very complicated beings with many different levels and centers. When a negative emotion is active, it wants 100 percent of our attention. In that way, it keeps us asleep. The moment we put part of our attention somewhere else, the negative emotion loses some of its power.

If an enraged woman tries to control her anger directly, she usually gets more angry. Many people have discovered an indirect method: counting to ten. That simple exercise helps because the effort put into counting takes away some of the energy that was put into the anger. Instead of trying to control her anger, the woman wakes up to that part of herself that is not angry and can calmly count to ten. When she wakes up, the anger loses some of its power.

Another way to do this is to focus your attention on something else. Some people do it by rubbing the back of their hand until they can feel a tingling or warmth. By putting attention onto the back of the hand, we give the emotion less attention, and it is free to subside. We call this act of focusing on the sensations in the hands "sensing." It is possible to put attention on the back of your hand even when you are doing something else. You can experiment with this by rubbing the back of your nondominant hand until it tingles. Then continue reading while keeping part of your awareness on your hand. You can divide your attention in that way.

With practice you can do this for several minutes or even hours. It is a skill that can be developed like any other skill. Its importance lies in giving you a tool to use when some negative emotion starts to overwhelm you.

If you notice yourself getting furious, you can divide your attention. In that divided state, only part of you is angry, and the other part is calmly observing. You are simply finding a calmer part of yourself so that you are not overwhelmed with anger. This is possible because there are many levels in the human mind.

Returning to the analogy of the mansion, it is like a person stuck in the basement, full of anger and deep in misery. Then a voice from one of the higher floors of the house calls down, "What are you doing down there?" The other voice is also a part of us; it is just on a higher level, and it calls our attention away from our misery.

Jesus told a parable that involved a son who received his inheritance and wasted it on riotous living until his money ran out and he was eating the food used for the pigs. At a certain point, he came to himself and began to reflect on the difference between his current life and the life of the hired servants in the house he left. He woke up to his situation (Luke 15).

Some of these wake-up calls are very dramatic and come at a desperate time in our lives. We can also wake up in those little moments when we are feeling frustrated, fearful, or just annoyed. That was what our spiritual-growth group discovered when they were directed to practice the first task:

THE FIRST TASK

When you notice a negative emotion, divide your attention. Put part of your attention on the back of your hand, keep it there while the emotion is going on, and notice any changes in the emotion. (Deep breathing or counting to ten can be substituted for the hand-rubbing technique as a means of dividing your attention.)

REPORTING ON THE TASK

Marie: I am so grateful that I'm actively working on spiritual growth, because it makes such a difference in our household. I was grieving the loss of my puppy. I think grief is a fine thing to feel, but what I noticed is that I didn't want to feel the grief. I used the technique with my hand to channel some of my attention away from the grief. I felt like I was experiencing the grief very soberly, and I was able to let it go after a time. I wasn't running away from it.

I had another experience where I took the kids and a friend to pick up tickets for a show. As soon as my friend got in the car, my daughter started screaming. We got to the pool and got my older daughter, and we got back in the car, and she started screaming again. I thought, "Well, she'll have to survive." And then she started screaming so much that she started throwing up in the back of the car. And then my other daughter started screaming, "Oh, what a disaster!" And I thought, "Back of my hand! Breathe!"

I'm in the middle of this traffic jam, and there's no way I'm going to get out, and there's throw-up all over the back of the car, all over my daughter. So I thought, "I've got to get out," and I eased through three lanes of traffic, parked the car, took my daughter out, cleaned her off. I'm thinking, "What am I going to do? If I put her back in, she's gonna scream again." In the past, I would get so mad and yell, or just be really resentful. But this time I was really aware, and laughing about it, and breathing. I thought, "What a great opportunity to work on the task."

Janet: I had to remind myself to start doing this task every day, and be diligent. I've been feeling a lot of guilt. I think it's the offshoot of depression. I'll start feeling guilt, or anger, or irritation. Then I'll remember to do the task. A couple of times I pinched my hand, but sometimes I just did the breathing; that was easier. When I did that, I found that I couldn't concentrate on the anger. It just pulled my attention away.

Klara: I thought about the task several times a day, every day. I didn't feel that I was particularly successful at the task. I kept thinking about it, thinking, "I need to do that." When the opportunity arose, I thought, "Yeah, I should do that." But I just ignored it. So I wrote in my journal about it.

I guess the best thing I got out of this week was recognizing my negative thoughts and realizing what I enjoy about them. So that was pretty helpful. It helped to diffuse my desire to continue feeling angry, vengeful, or self-righteous. I realized that, in the long run, I'm not doing myself any good.

Stewart: For me, my lower self loves to get going on trying to control outcomes that I really have no control over. Kids tend to really challenge me a lot. I had my two daughters for the evening by myself, and it was just before they were going to sleep. They needed to go to the bathroom one last time. My younger daughter's trying to be potty trained on a little plastic potty, and my elder daughter thinks it's interesting to use it. And it's mildly annoying, because you have to clean up the potty, and it's not necessary. So she sat down on the potty, and I said, "Please don't do that. I would really prefer if you didn't do that, because then I have to clean it out again, and I've done it a couple of times today." And she said, "No, I really need to use the little potty."

And then, I don't know what went wrong—the angle was wrong or something—but when she urinated, it just sprayed out all over her sister's pajamas, over the walls, it bounced off the toilet seat. There was urine everywhere, and I got so angry. I didn't even have time to focus on my hand or anything. There was no time; I was so annoyed that she didn't listen to me. And I got mad, and I could see myself out of control, and I could see how scary that would be for the child.

I said, "Back away! Just back away!" I was trying to get control over the situation, although it was already out of control. I said, "Back away, go toward the sink and start washing your feet in the sink!" So I got it all cleaned up, and it occurred to me that, really, I could have gone through the same experience—if I hadn't been trying to control my daughter, if I'd just watched it all happen. She felt so bad; she just was so scared. And I thought, "Wow, you know, it was an accident, and my lower self turned it into this thing where I resented her for it."

Just then my wife came home, and that kind of threw me off because I was just about to make amends and apologize to everyone. My wife took the kids, so I had to be by myself for half an hour after all that. It was really interesting, because I had to come back to the breath, and I ended up doing some reading that I had wanted to do.

But that was my big failure. It wasn't a real failure; it was an opportunity to grow. But I noticed how quickly sometimes you need to invoke the task.

Frank: I've been having a battle with a government agency for about four years now. They think I'm making much more money than I'm making. As flattering as that is, it's hard when they dock us money. So finally we talked to a person who said, "Hmm, I think you have a point. Just send us certain pages from your income tax returns for the following years." So I finally got around to doing it and couldn't find one of the years. "Where did I put it?" It wasn't in the briefcase where I thought it was, and it wasn't in the tax file where it should have been. And I noticed my lower self getting real worked up about this and feeling frantic. I was kicking myself for not filing things properly.

Then I thought, "When in doubt, do the task." I put the attention on the back of my hand and calmed myself down, and then realized that there was another person in the room who wasn't upset. I said, "Would you see if you can find it?" And every time my mind raced with the thought, "I've lost it forever," and all those crazy thoughts, I just put my attention on the back of my hand and calmed down. In about ten minutes, this other person walked in the room, with the papers in hand. No big deal. My lower self wanted to make a huge deal out of it.

Elly: Almost as soon as I left here, one thing after another happened. I had people coming in from out of town, unexpected guests and family. I was glad for the task because I really was, at one point, able to step away from it and relax. I felt grateful because there are certain things that *weren't* going wrong, and I was just holding onto those.

Bob: I had a good occasion to use the task when I became an unwilling participant in a political discussion this week. My views are somewhat conservative, and I found myself among the most vehement liberals I have ever encountered. It was all I could do to hold my tongue and my temper as these people purposely worked on me, making light of my viewpoints on many subjects. I resorted to rubbing the back of my hand while biting my tongue to keep from lashing out.

Session Leader: Notice how the lower self likes to upset you. Ordinarily we could look at something like a slow driver and just say, "Oh, he's driving slowly." The lower self wants to make a case out of it. "Agh! Look at that! He's a menace to society!"

Now suppose, instead of the driver, we talk about a person who has political views other than our own. It's no different than the driver in the sense that there are people who hold one position and there are people who hold another position.

The lower self wants to make a case out of it. The lower self likes to play, and it's always looking for reasons to get us upset. "There is a conservative!" "Can you imagine?" "Look at that flaming liberal!"

It doesn't matter what it is. You go to a meeting of people from a political party that you do not support, and you *know* the opinions being expressed will be other than those you hold. The lower self loves this, because it then has a reason to spend the evening being indignant. But the fact is that we do not have to react that way. It's wonderful to have a tool to deal with our negative responses.

TASK 2
Dealing with Difficult Emotions

Lead my soul out of prison, to acknowledge your name.
Psalm 142:7

SOMETIMES WE FIND OURSELVES in a bad mood, but have no idea how to get out of it. We try to change our own state of mind, but it doesn't work. If someone else comes along and tries to cheer us up, we feel even worse. It's as if the bad mood locks us into a kind of spiritual prison.

You have probably noticed how hard it is to talk someone out of their emotions, or even to control your own emotions. Feelings do not respond to direct commands. It is as if they do not understand words. If words don't help, what can we do when we are in a negative state?

We have two distinct aspects to our inner life, the thinking side and the feeling side. Both are important. Without thoughts, we would be unconscious. Without feelings, we would be lifeless. Both of these aspects can be negative or positive.

Negative feelings include such emotions as fear, hatred, jealousy, self-pity, depression, contempt of others, and hopelessness. Positive feelings include such emotions as peace, contentment, joy, excitement, caring, patience, and love. Notice that some of these feelings are very powerful, and some of them are potentially destructive. Learning how to deal with them is one of our greatest challenges as human beings, especially since they have such a profound effect on our relationships with other people.

Thoughts can also be positive or negative. "Life is good," "We can deal with this," "You are a worthwhile person," and "My life has meaning" are some positive ones. Negative thoughts sound more like this: "I am no good," "Nothing makes sense," "All people are miserable and selfish," "Everyone treats me badly," "No one understands me," and so on. When I was a child, we summarized this all in the little ditty: "Nobody likes me. Everybody hates me. I'm going to eat worms and die." When we felt really bad, we would continue: "Big fat greasy ones, long thin smelly ones, horrible little ugly ones, I'm going to eat worms and die."

Thoughts and feelings are interconnected, as if they are married to each other. When the thoughts and feelings are positive, it makes for a happy marriage. When the feelings are miserable and the thoughts negative, it makes for an infernal marriage. In the diagram on page 19, you see arrangements of large and small arrows. The large arrows in the center of each circle represent feelings. Arrows pointing upward represent positive feelings. Those pointing downward are negative feelings. Each large arrow is surrounded by a cluster of smaller arrows. These represent the thoughts that surround and support our feelings.

Of the four circles, two are labeled as "stable arrangements" because the large and small arrows are going in the same direction. Two are unstable, because there is a contradiction between the direction of the large arrow and the smaller ones.

In the diagrams of stable arrangements, an arrow pointing upward represents a positive feeling, and the cluster of little arrows pointing in the same direction represents the many positive thoughts that support the feeling. For example, if you are feeling good about yourself, the large arrow is pointing upward. You will then have thoughts that are positive: "Life is good," "I am a worthwhile person," "I like what I am doing, and I do it well," "Other people respect me," and so on.

When the large arrow is pointing downward, it represents a negative emotion, such as self-pity. The negative thoughts surrounding it sound like this: "I am a failure," "No one cares about me," "I can't do anything right."

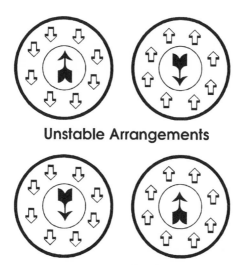

Unstable Arrangements

Stable Arangements

Then there are the unstable positions. They are labeled "unstable" because they cannot stay that way for long. The large and small arrows will eventually tend to line up with each other. Even if you are feeling positive, a cluster of negative thoughts can eventually drag you down to the point where you end up feeling negative.

There is an old British vaudeville song in which the words say "By George, you do look well" for a few verses, and it's clear the person in the song feels great during this time. Then it shifts, and the message is "By George, you do look ill." In no time, it's clear the person feels terrible. This shows the power of thoughts to trigger emotions.

We cannot control our emotions directly. The large arrow is beyond our control. We do have control over our thoughts, however, and this gives us a very powerful tool in our own spiritual life. If we know we are in a bad mood, we can shift our attention to our thoughts and do what we can to change them. By changing our thoughts, we can indirectly move the large arrow representing our emotions.

Suppose we are feeling dejected and bad about ourselves. Instead of reciting the little ditty about how nobody loves us, we can amend the words. We can reflect on the fact that we really do not know how other people see us, and that there are people who love us. We can say that eating worms and dying isn't going to make people love us, and besides, those worms are probably a much healthier diet than the food we normally put in our mouths.

We have powerful levers in those small arrows. If we can manage to keep our mind dwelling on positive thoughts even for a few minutes, we will experience a change in the negative emotion. The negative emotion cannot survive without its surrounding cluster of negative thoughts. If those thoughts are replaced by positive ones, the negative emotion simply vanishes, at least for a time.

There is much talk about the need to honor and express our feelings. We have seen the consequences of people repressing their feelings. What is the difference between this task and repressing emotions?

Emotions are a very important of our life. It is important to be in touch with them and to honor them. There are many times when emotions give us important signals. Anger might inspire us to correct some injustice. Fear might help us to avoid danger. But more often, a negative emotion has no positive value. Feeling hatred toward someone has no positive use. Self-pity does nothing to improve our life. Many kinds of fear cripple us without adding anything useful to our life. In a sense, negative emotions are like uncomfortable feelings in the body. Once a toothache has inspired us to get dental care, it is of no value to us.

Although it has positive uses, as we have just seen, pain is a negative experience. We naturally seek relief from pain. The same can be said for negative emotions. They may have value to us as signals of greater distress, but they are terrible to live with, and we want relief from them.

ANGER

Anger is of special interest. When we were children, many of us were told not to be angry. We might have been punished for being angry. As a result, we learned not to express anger and maybe not even to feel it. Some people in therapy experience a breakthrough when they finally get in touch with their anger, express it, and let it go. This is a healthy thing to do. This does not mean, however, that being chronically angry is a healthy thing. Recent studies have shown that anger is very destructive, and can lead to violence, abuse, and murder. Even if it's not acted upon, anger causes harm to our own bodies by increasing blood pressure, affecting digestion, and causing a host of other problems.

Chronically angry people do not need to be told that their anger is fine, and that it is healthy to express it. They need to know how to reduce it or get rid of it.

Sometimes this involves taking some kind of action, but very often, it simply requires internal spiritual work, and for that we need tools. The exercise of replacing negative thoughts with positives ones can be a very powerful means of reducing anger. Take this example: A woman is driving along a road, and another driver cuts in front of her, almost causing an accident. This triggers a number of emotions, especially fear and anger. The upset woman can dwell on the event and intensify the anger with such internal messages as "That fool has no consideration for other people," "Drivers like that should be shot," "Wouldn't it be great if he had an accident and got killed?" "Nobody has any consideration these days." The anger surrounds itself with negative thoughts like this that swirl around in a person's head, increasing her anger almost to the boiling point.

A person doing spiritual work would handle the situation differently. When the driver cuts in front of the woman, the fear and anger she initially feels would be the same as for anyone else. Her mind would also begin its internal muttering, but the person, noticing the negative pattern, would take steps to improve the situation. She would acknowledge the fear and anger, and also be aware of the stream of negative thoughts. She would then make a conscious effort to replace the negative thoughts with positive ones.

We might think that we cannot come up with any positive thoughts for such a situation, but it is important that we do. If the anger is not reduced, it could lead us to take some reckless action, or eat us away on the inside. The spiritual person turns to thoughts such as "Isn't it wonderful that we didn't collide," "That person must be very relieved that he didn't kill someone," "I am glad that I am a careful driver," "That other driver might have had a very difficult day. Maybe he just got fired. I hope his day improves."

But aren't we making things up? Yes, we are. But remember, we are always making things up about other people: "She probably doesn't like me," "He probably waited to cut in front of me and not some other car," "He probably always cuts in front of women drivers," and so on. Any thought we have about the other driver is mostly fiction. Why not make it nice fiction?

If that sounds like being unrealistic, think of the results. The negative thoughts lead to negative emotions and usually to negative actions often with dire consequences. The positive thoughts lead to positive actions, more consideration for others, and better feelings. Isn't it more realistic to deal with the situation in a way that makes it better, and not worse? We can do that when we use our power to create positive mental images in a way that will reduce negative emotions and maximize positive ones.

WHAT ABOUT GRIEF?

Is grief a negative emotion? By itself, grief is just a natural response to loss. When you lose something, it hurts. However, grief easily gets infected with negative emotions. It is the most prone to infection of any of our emotions. When a person is grieving, he or she is open to anger, guilt, and self-pity. These emotions are opportunistic, like certain diseases that attack us when we are physically low. And there are a lot of other negative emotions that can go in and infect the grief wound.

Grief is a wound of the spirit that can be compared with a physical wound. If a person cuts his finger, the first thing to do is put on some kind of antibiotic ointment, and then bandage the wound to prevent it from getting infected. The bandage does not heal the wound; it simply protects the area during the natural process of healing. Time, then, can heal the wound.

The same is true with grief. If we lose a loved one through death, or for some reason are separated from loved ones, it hurts. It is not healthy to deny the hurt or ignore it. It is normal to cry as a way of dealing with the pain. Some people find it helpful to share their feelings with someone else. It is not necessary to do spiritual work on grief because it is a natural and healthy process.

But when a person is grieving, there is a need to protect against the secondary infections of negative emotions. For example, if a man who has suffered a loss feels self-pity or resentment, he can work on those things. He can change his thinking about them, find some positive thing to think instead, and still let himself grieve.

Here, then, is a second spiritual task.

THE SECOND TASK

When you become aware of a negative emotion in yourself, notice what thoughts come with it. If you have a negative thought, observe the emotions that come with it and how quick they are to arrive. When you are conscious of an active negative emotion, experiment with stopping the negative thoughts surrounding it. Notice any changes in the negative emotions.

REPORTING ON THE TASK

Bob: This is a little thing, but it often happens to me. I get impatient when I get caught in traffic. Negative thoughts about those "idiots" who can't drive come bubbling up from my basement.

While I was driving to work this week, I was caught on a winding road behind an old lady doing no more than twenty miles per hour. There was nowhere to pass, so I was forced to follow her at her snail's pace. Immediately, the thought "This old bag is going to make me late" came into my mind. I could feel the tension begin to make the muscles in my back stiffen. My emotions were even taking control of my body.

I remembered the task and tried to stop the negative thought about being late for work. In truth, I had plenty of time, and the little old lady could block my way for only a few more minutes. The tension left my back muscles. My thoughts changed to admiration for a very old lady who had the guts to get out on her own in rush-hour traffic. The task worked for me on this recurring negative emotion.

Keri: I was having a bad day, and I stayed longer at lunch talking to someone than I was supposed to. I came back and there's a note on my desk saying, "Please see me, D," and D's the administrator. So I thought, "Well, maybe, I should say, 'I know I was late.' Maybe that's what she wants." Many negative things were bouncing back and forth in my head, and I was trying to imagine the best. And then she comes up to me, and she says, "Congratulations! You won the raffle!" It turned out that I'd won the raffle to the zoo from a fund-raiser.

So I thought that I was imagining the best, but I wasn't. I really imagined the worst. I could have thought, "I'll be the one who won the raffle," but I didn't think that.

Noomay: I had a hard time because I couldn't find the paper with the task on it. I was just watching my thoughts. It was almost harder, because there were no consequences outside of myself. When I start thinking negative things, I start feeling bad about myself. At different times I would say, "Oh yeah, the task!" Then I would get in a better mood, and actually enjoy the moment that I was in, and start to be able to breathe easily, and think of special things and special people. It seemed too easy to just continue the negative thoughts and the worry.

Janet: I am having a hard time with some of the bigger things that are going on in my life. I really want some changes to be made. I'd think, "Oh, I'm too scared to do that," or "I'm not strong enough,"or "What's the use?" I have a really negative focus. I hate that, because I've been stuck in that over the years. I stay in the negative place forever because of fear. I couldn't sleep last night, and I remembered to relax, and I could feel all this tension around my eyes. I should talk through this with my therapist.

Session Leader: When you're in that helpless mode, there's certain thought patterns that get you going. It's hard to reverse those thoughts.

Darren: As some of you know, I'm getting married. And this week, the sheer terror of that fact arose. It's arisen about three times, and even in the heat of the terror, two things were clear to me. Every other thought was negative. I'm definitely glad to be getting married to the person I'm marrying.

I was going through terrors like "Oh, what is this all about? What am I getting into?" I was cleaning up the house, and I found this task sheet, so I read it, and I thought, "Okay. I'm going through terror. I'm not going to think." And as soon as I said that, I could see thoughts just whizzing by, and they were all thoughts of "Make a decision, make it now, end it!" There was an urgency in the thoughts: "You've gotta get out! You've gotta get out! This isn't right! End, end, end, end, end!"

So instead of having the thoughts and grabbing on to them, I just started observing them. And I realized the feeling I was in was kind of just like swimming in the water, and the water was getting rough. Every thought was like an anchor, a weight taking me down and trying to make me sink. And the thoughts' total intent was to destroy something very special to me.

By not identifying myself with those thoughts, I was able to rethink, "Well, you know, this isn't actually the worst feeling." The thoughts are really defining the feeling as a terrible, hopeless thing; but when I dropped the thoughts, I realized it was much more harmless than I thought. But my negative thoughts would come and go, and then I would totally identify with them. I'd go back and forth, and it was a constant battle, but it was a really good exercise for me. I really think it enabled me to get out of the mode more quickly.

Session Leader: You know the parable of the wheat and the tares in the New Testament? When the farmer found tares among the wheat, he said, "Hmm, an enemy has done this." I think this is so unusual. Imagine working in your garden, seeing weeds and saying, "An enemy has done this." But if you start noticing these thoughts, it is an enemy of your peace. All these thoughts do is drag you down. So simply not believing the thoughts is an important form of self-defense.

Greg: I found that my negative thoughts were on two very different levels of intensity. There are ones that were very easily banished. I engaged those very successfully. But then I was sometimes conscious of the fact that negative thoughts come in waves, and these are harder to dismiss.

I finally cottoned to the idea that there was an emotion underlying the thoughts. The important thing was not the negative thought. It was the emotion that was fueling this flood, because isolated negative thoughts are very easily dealt with.

Others were much more difficult. For example, I have been experiencing negative thoughts about a writing project I'm working on. They are fueled by a fear of failure. I had this exhilarating experience last week of real breakthrough. I was going to be able to carry this thing through. But no sooner was that in place, no sooner did I have a sense of seeing the road mapped out even though I haven't walked it yet, than there came a flood of doubts: "Well, okay, you've done this much, you've seen the road, but will you be able to really walk it? Will you be able to execute it?"

I'm not so sure I really combated that very successfully. My approach was basically to doggedly dig in and pursue the tasks rather than, say, stepping back and watching the flight of the negative thought. I sort of got in there and said, "Well, I'll show you!" And I had a couple of episodes over the course of the week where I basically worked hard rather than smart, worked too long, should have slowed down and changed my focus. So I had rather checkered success with dealing with the flood of negative thoughts that were surrounding a sense of real pleasure in a task.

Session Leader: These thoughts, of course, have different feelings altogether than the positive feelings.

Greg: Absolutely. It's all about not being able to do it. If everything gets helter-skelter, time is rushing by. Things that ought to be manageable are not. You feel a sense of urgency that's just frustrating your ability to concentrate and manage.

Darren: Can I add one more thing that came up for me? I really understand now that when I identify with negative thoughts, my life becomes unmanageable. I look at my life from the perspective of those thoughts, and my life looks terrible and hopeless. So it quickly becomes completely irrational, and I become truly helpless because of my identification with the negative thoughts.

Klara: I ended up at the same place this week as last week. I haven't done the task right, and it wasn't working. I was sort of judging myself because I was thinking, "Well, I didn't really do anything with the negative thoughts. I sort of rode with them and watched them march by." But toward the end of the week, I realized that this approach was probably the right thing for me to do. It was not exactly what the task was really calling for, but I felt detached from the negative thoughts. Maybe because I was more aware, when a negative thought would come up, I went, "Uh oh! A negative thought!" And I'd sort of just let myself go through with the emotion that flowed from that thought. "Um, so it's a negative thought. Okay. Anger. Of course, yes, I'm angry about that." Then I felt properly detached.

Session Leader: I just want to draw attention to the different ways that this task can be done. One of them you mentioned is to observe the thoughts walking by or flowing in, or whatever image you use. To become an observer of them instead of totally being overwhelmed by them gives some freedom. Another way is to disbelieve them. You can observe them and still sort of believe them, but if you observe them and say, "It's all lies," that gives you another freedom. The third thing to do is to just stop the thoughts. That's hard to do; these thoughts have an energy of their own, but if you can have some thoughts going through and just turn them off, then of course the negative emotions don't have any source of power to live off. A fourth way is to replace them, to replace them continually. A negative thought comes in, you replace it with a positive thought—again and again.

Frank: I've had several experiences with the task, but the one I'm going to talk about has to do with Sunday night television. There was a TV program about a person who had witnessed a crime but did nothing to stop it. I did not see the program or read anything about the case. I was told about the program and a related magazine article by a significant person in my life.

The program and article were about a person who witnessed rape and murder and didn't do anything to stop it.

Sunday night, they interviewed this guy. In the interview, he had no sense of repentance about it. Well, when I start to think about this, I get all kinds of feelings: "I could murder the guy. Throw him in jail, throw away the key." And then I just noticed, all these thoughts are really a kind of fiction. I've never met the guy. It's a story that happened a long time ago. It's second-, third-, or fourth-hand. I did not read the article in a magazine; I didn't watch the program on TV. It's just someone else telling me about something that she has read and something she saw on TV. And my negative emotions are loving it! I've never even heard of him before. I have nothing to do with him.

So I just thought, "I can't believe all these negative thoughts and let them dwell in my mind. Just get them out of there and replace them with something else." And the thought came in: "If I knew something about this situation, I might feel differently. My feelings are not based on the truth; they are based on the fact that I want to feel angry at somebody, and this guy's a great example of someone you can really hate!"

It's all to do with my lower self and nothing to do with this guy. He's going to be judged; I don't have to be his judge and executor. It really took a conscious effort to shift my train of thought onto something that did not have so many attach points for negative emotions. It's a very sad story, but it's not an excuse for my hate monsters to run around and make me miserable.

Klara: I felt like I was really resisting this task and as a result, ending up facing the reality of how much I love negative thoughts! I love what I get out of them. I feel that was really a freeing experience because, it's like, after I said, "I love it, and you can't make me stop," then it was okay. And this week I felt a lot more detached.

Session Leader: This is a very important point: We talk as if we don't like these negative things, but part of us does.

Darren: I have one more thing. Someone said, "Success is very easy. All you have to do is not shoot yourself in the foot." I notice with these thoughts, they're just like, "Come on! Do it! Do it! Shoot yourself in the foot!" One thing that's really helped me my whole life is what my dad has always told me, "Never make the decision from a negative thought." And I always want to, in the most urgent way, make a decision. It's all based on shooting myself in the foot and a false reality that could trap me and it might be too late. It's always been useful for me to keep that in mind.

Greg: I did find a very useful antidote was to try to inject some play into what I was doing. I sort of do the mental equivalent of finger-painting. Here's what I did specifically: I was working on a project that involves a lot of maps and information, and I'd get up and abandon the frustration that was going on and basically push color-headed pins in a map. It was a task that needed to be done, but it also had a certain element of the absurd. It was a tiny and very manageable task, but it would remind me of the thing that made it all worth doing and a wonderful project in the first place. For me, there's a very strong sense of rediscovering the element of play. I find it's very centering just to get that distance from what's frustrating me and see the element of comedy and silliness in much of the serious things I find myself involved in.

Session Leader: Yes, the beasts in the basement don't like it when you play. They want you to take life seriously.

Marie: I was working at it really hard. A negative emotion would come up I would look at the negative thoughts and try to turn them into positive thoughts. But then it would start this argument in my head. And the more I would try and figure out positive thoughts, the more my lower self would argue, and she would win. Then I thought, "Okay, this is not working." Then I tried just giving up on it, forgetting that thought and just being in the moment, and that seemed to work a lot better for me. Just stop thinking about it and just realize where I am and what's going on around me.

Stewart: I did a lot of fall cleaning, trying to fix all the things that need fixing in this huge house. I borrowed a ladder. I needed to do some things way up high, and every time I was climbing up the ladder, my little one-year-old would just climb up after me. She'd come right up to where I was. I'd have to climb down and put her down, and she'd get up. If I turned around for a second, she'd be halfway up the ladder. It just drove me nuts! I couldn't even go down to get a wrench!

I started getting really frustrated, thinking "I can't do anything today! It just has to be done!" But then I figured out that I needed to find something that she loves doing. I gave her some soapy water and a scrub brush. She scrubbed the floors, the chairs. She had so much fun, and I thought, "There you go!"

So that was the thing for me, having the thought, "Well, just find something on the list that can be done, get rid of that horrible overwhelming feeling."

Nicole: I'm having a hard time with thoughts and emotions. There was one thing that sticks out the most. I was worried about health issues. We talked before about what thoughts or emotions tend to come up. I knew that fear was definitely one of them. I was letting my mind go and thinking about the worst possible consequences. Sometimes during the week, I was all right. But then I find I'd be all worried. So I didn't actually feel completely better until I went to the doctor and found out everything's fine.

Session Leader: When there's something like that pending, and you really need to go to the doctor, the spiritual work can only take you so far. But after doing the spiritual work, you will be in a more balanced state of mind and better able to make good decisions.

TASK 3

Identifying with Positive Emotions

If people believed, as is the truth, that everything good and true comes from the Lord and everything evil and false comes from hell, they wouldn't take goodness in as their own and feel they deserve a reward for it, and they wouldn't take evil in as their own and make themselves guilty of it.

Emanuel Swedenborg, *Divine Providence* 320

THERE ARE TIMES when we feel overwhelmed by events in our lives. There are times when we become swamped with negative emotions. We might be paralyzed by fear, choked with anger, or green with jealousy. In these situations, it is as if our whole attention is focused on the emotion, and it seems we have little or no power to escape from it. These are the situations where the technique of "non-identification" can be very helpful. As the name suggests, we can become too identified with our feelings. If that happens, we become snared by them.

THE MONKEY TRAP

Consider the monkey trap. It is a very simple device for catching monkeys, just a hollow coconut or jar full of peanuts tied to a tree. The opening to the coconut is so small that the monkey can fit its hand in when it is empty, but can't pull it out when it is full. To catch a monkey, you just put the coconut where the monkey will find it. It sees the peanuts, puts its hand in and grabs a handful of peanuts. Now its hand is so big the monkey can't pull it out. Unwilling to let go of the peanuts, the monkey is trapped.

In our case, we are not clinging to peanuts, but negative emotions. Our problems come not because we have negative feelings, but because we *identify* ourselves with them and become attached to them. We won't let go.

Imagine yourself walking into a parking lot. You see a car hit another vehicle and then drive off. You find yourself thinking some negative thoughts and feelings about hit-and-run drivers. And then you notice that the car that has been hit is *your* car. Can you imagine how different you feel?

The difference comes because of the way you identify with your possessions. Otherwise, you could just say, "A car has been hit and its owner must fix it." But if it's *your* car, your reactions are much more intense. You feel hurt, insulted, violated, furious.

Imagine that you were attached to your favorite armchair, so that wherever you went, you had to take it with you, glued to your body. What if you could not go anywhere without it being attached to you? You could move, but only with great difficulty, and you could never get out of your house. It's hard to carry that much baggage around. But what about your emotional baggage?

We eventually realize that we are not our clothes, or any other of our possessions, and this is important to our sense of well-being. Otherwise, we couldn't imagine life without those possessions. When we identify with anything, we limit our own spiritual growth. Some of our freedom is lost. We may think our emotions are us, but they are not.

THE BASEMENT OR THE ATTIC?

If you look at the diagram of the house, you will see all kinds of things in the basement. These are no more you than your furniture or your car. They are just things that enter you, and they can

enter through the slightest cracks. If you identify with them and
say things like "I'm angry," "I'm worried," "I'm a very nervous person," and so on, then you are in the monkey trap. These negative emotions will begin to dominate your life.

The House

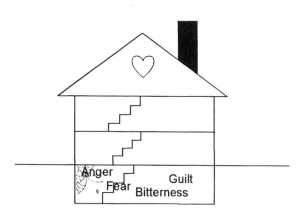

The beasts in the basement

Some people find it very hard to separate their feelings from
their sense of who they are. Some have learned how to dissociate from their feelings to the point where they are out of touch
with them. This usually happens to children when they have had
to cope with some extremely difficult and painful situation, such
as having an alcoholic parent or being abused. Their survival may
depend on being able to dissociate from their experience: "This
is not happening to me." But later in life, this distance from their
own emotions can cause many problems. They may need therapy to help them get in touch with their emotions.

Excellent work is being done by some therapists to help such
adults get in touch with their anger. These individuals are invited
to hit a pillow and scream to the point where the full extent of
their anger comes to the surface and can be deeply felt. In a sense,

they have to almost *become* their anger to release long-repressed feelings. Once that work has been done, they can move on to the kind of task discussed in this chapter where they admit their anger and then dissociate from it. All we need to do is to dissociate: "These emotions are going on in me, but they are not me."

This task is also important to use with positive emotions on the upper levels. They aren't us either. They come from the life that flows into us. Take the feeling of love toward our neighbors. If we identify with that love, how can we avoid the trap of conceit or selfish pride?

If we could only operate on the principle that we are vessels that receive life and that everything flows into us, we would be truly and wonderfully free. Then we would be able to observe the good things in us and thank God for them. At the same time, when we became aware of some of those ugly beasts in our basement, we would not be overwhelmed. We would be aware that they are there, but they are not us, either.

This even applies to physical illness. When we say "my arthritis" or "my heart trouble," we are somehow attaching ourselves to our aches and pains. Couldn't it be nicer to say, "My body has arthritis, but I don't"?

It can be hard to define exactly who and what we are as human beings. There are many aspects of our life, but these do not define who we are. We have many material possessions that are nice to have, but they are not us. These physical things come and go. Most people live in at least four different houses during their lifetimes, and own a dozen or so different cars. The possessions are there for a time. We enjoy them and we identify with them, but they are not us.

The same can be said for our passing moods and feelings. They all are an important part of our lives, but we are not our possessions, we are not our bodies, we are not our feelings or our thoughts. We are more of a spiritual essence within and above all of these things, and no matter what may be going on in our conscious thoughts and feelings, our true inner self is always at peace.

To lessen the hold that negative emotions can have on us, we can do a simple task called non-identification.

THE THIRD TASK

When you become aware of a negative emotion in yourself, say, "*It* is (fill in the effect of the emotion, such as angry, hurt, fearful, etc.), and I don't have to be." Notice the results.

REPORTING ON THE TASK

Marie: Sunday I was really sick. We went out to my friend's house with the girls and my husband. I said, "Well, I'm not going to do anything 'cause I'm really sick with this strep throat. But then I ended up taking the girls out because they were being really loud and obnoxious so nobody could talk. So then I was doing my martyr thing that I always do, like "Oh, *I'll* do it!" And then I was sitting there with the girls, thinking, "I can't believe I'm sitting here, and I'm the one that's sick and my husband's in there, and he's well. He should be in here!" And then I thought, "Oh you know, this is all lies. "*It* is upset, and I don't have to be." And I just started letting go and looking at where I was. I was lying there on the couch and didn't have to do anything. The girls were playing happily, and I thought, "Oh, I see. I get to see my kids play," and it just totally changed my state of mind.

Klara: This is a concept I grew up with and was familiar with: The idea that we don't own evil thoughts, that your evil thoughts are not you. And that's something that I really believe in. But I did find that I don't practice that on a day-to-day basis, even though I know it to be true and it makes a lot of sense to me.

I find that I only use that approach when I get a real winger coming through, something really bad, and I think "Whoa! I can identify *that* as not being my thought." But day-to-day stuff is a lot more difficult not to own, because I just feel responsible and feel these things, and I am them. So the little sentence was really helpful: "*It* is [blank], and I don't have to be." I found that very helpful. "It" was really tangible, to just say, "*It* is doing this, and *it* feels this way. *It* wants this to happen."

It was kind of fun in a way, because I could be very specific, like, "*It* wants to be damaging. *It* wants this other person to know how badly it feels. *It* wants them to squirm." It was very helpful to use the "*it*," and then I really put *it* outside of myself.

Darren: When I said, "*It* is angry," I really was speaking of an energy outside of myself flowing through. And then to call *it* "that anger," not myself, is really an interesting concept.

There was this lady who came to visit; she heard about me, and she also does yoga. She was traveling, and she came to stay with me. I noticed that I became intensely critical of her and was very blocked off. I had an attitude that sort of said, "Do your own thing, and don't bother me. You can stay here, but just don't talk to me." She was nothing but kind, considerate, and friendly. So I would talk about it to my fiancée when we're driving in the car. It was like, "Yeah, you know, I am just powerless to these feelings of being critical to her."

So what I really got to was that the only way I'm going to detach is if I really believe "it" isn't me, I can say with words, "*It* isn't angry," but I really have to get, "This anger is not me," which is not so easy for me.

Lusting is a good example; there's definitely a shame attached to that kind of emotion. So if I go, "*It* is lusting," I really don't believe that. And because I don't believe it, I appropriate it to myself, and then the guilt of that becomes what attaches it to me. And so I can also say, "*It* is lusting, and *it* is now guilty, and *it* is believing that it is me." And I found myself saying *it* constantly. "*It* is angry; now *it* is lusting; now *it* is upset." It was like, "Boy, this *it* is, seems like, 98 percent. Who am I, the two percent?" So that was a pretty odd experience. But all in all, somehow it was positive, overwhelming as it was.

Noomay: I started off the week with a dream that I had about someone. In the dream the person said, "You're a loser." And I remember the task coming in, and I said to myself, "*It* is angry; I don't have to be." And so I talked to her, told her, "I wanted to get back in touch with you; I'm sorry I left." I just felt like it was very powerful, when I woke up, that the task was actually in my subconscious. It seemed to really help me throughout the week when different things would come up. I was watching some program that was really upsetting. Difficult things came up and brought up emotions in me that were just wacko and completely unrelated. And I would say it again, "*It* is angry, but I am sad. "I couldn't quite get it out, but it did help me change it. It helped me to just sort of turn it into a prayer.

The hardest ones were more direct relationship situations where I felt out of control. Certain planning things came up; I just felt totally out of control, and I would repeat "*It* is out of control, but I don't have to be." But then I didn't really feel it, and I would say the phrase again and again. But just by saying "it" was sort of amusing to me and kind of broke the control that the negative emotions were having over me. Just today my fiancé and I were singing in the car, "*It* is angry, but I don't have to be." It's sort of catchy. It really stuck in my head and was useful.

Frank: Today I was doing some work with the copier, and sometimes I get kind of anxious and irritated with the machine. "Why doesn't it work?" So I thought, "Better do the task. *It* is annoyed, but I don't have to be. *It* is impatient." I notice the anxiety would go down a little bit, but not totally disappear. And then I went back to the other task, because the thought that was supporting the impatience was, "I haven't got time." And I just said to myself: "Yep, after you finish this task, you'll go read the newspaper. Or you can just go play solitaire. And so you think that you have to get this done, and you're kind of annoyed it's taking longer than you want. But really you've got nothing else to do for a couple of hours." I could see how much I would believe this thought that I had to rush, rush, rush. But I find it sort of gets in my gut, this impatience and irritation with machines. And though the emotion reduced, it didn't go away entirely. It didn't get to the point where it was totally gone.

Angus: I had a strange week also. I reached a pretty low point. I thought the task was an interesting concept, but I didn't really internalize it. I think I had a real revelation when I was driving around. I felt like it explained a lot of things to me. It was like all the stuff that's happened is not what I want. It's me thinking that I'm "it." I feel like I always had this confusion between things, like what I want out of a relationship and things that I want from life. And then the "it" thing seemed like it explained things a little bit. Sometimes my human nature thwarts what I really want to do and be. So I felt this huge separation. That was good.

Bob: I don't want to offend anyone, but this task was so hard for me that I had to invent a technique to separate myself from "it." I gave my anger a name. I called it "Bob." That helped me identify my true self as something different from my anger.

When I observed myself getting angry, I simply said, "That is Bob. It's not me." Silly as it sounds, this technique allowed me to break the identity with my anger. It was then easy for me to separate my anger from the rest of me.

Session Leader: You got the message, Bob. The task is designed to make you feel separated from your emotions. When you achieve some separation, the emotions have much less power over you.

TASK 4

Letting Go of Criticism

Stop judging, so that you won't be judged. The judgment you pass will be passed on you, and the measurement you use will be used on you. Why are you looking at the wood sliver in your sibling's eye but not noticing the load-bearing beam in your own eye? Or how are you going to say to your sibling, "Let me get the sliver out of your eye," and look, there is a beam in your own eye? You hypocrite, first get the beam out of your eye, and then you will see clearly enough to get the sliver out of your sibling's eye.

Matthew 7:1–5

You are inexcusable, all you people passing judgment. For while you are judging the other person you are judging yourself; for you, the one judging, are doing the same things.

Romans 2:1

Those who have kindness hardly see any evil in others. They notice everything good and true in them; and they put a good interpretation on anything evil or false. All angels are this way, a trait they have from the Lord, who bends everything evil into good.

Emanuel Swedenborg, *Arcana Coelestia* 1079

IT IS HARD to grow spiritually if your thoughts of other people are harsh and critical. Put another way, if we want to grow spiritually, we need to let go of criticism.

What would happen if you were suddenly given the power to listen in on the inner dialogue of other people? Imagine having that power and going into a lunchroom of some office, what would you hear? "Look at what she's wearing!" "I can't stand the way he talks about himself so much." Things like that go on in people's heads all the time.

Now imagine a machine that was writing down your inner monologue as you were thinking it. Can you picture yourself reading through a transcript of your own stream of thoughts? Now take the transcript and highlight all of the thoughts that are critical. What percentage of your thoughts would be highlighted? It might be pretty high.

What would it be like for someone else to read a word-for-word document of all of the thoughts as they come into your head? After a while, they would probably drop the manuscript and say, "Don't you ever get bored with your own thoughts? I notice that whenever you see Fred, you mentally say the same critical things about him. Can't you think of something else to think? I would hate to live in your brain. Your thoughts sound like a broken record."

As I drive around town, I notice billboards. There is one that I can hardly look at without being critical. I don't like the artwork, and I don't like the product being advertised. How many times do I have to say in my head, "I don't like that billboard"? When I say it, who am I helping, anyway? Me? Yet every time I drive by, my mind gets into its criticism: "Ha! Humph! That billboard again! Humph! Why don't they get a new artist?" That kind of thought pattern is really boring. The monologue just goes round and round endlessly and purposelessly.

Somehow, we think that we are obliged to criticize, and if we stopped, the world would go to hell. Sometimes we feel that it is our duty to criticize others and point out where they are wrong. But does our criticism do anybody any good?

If I am talking to someone and put my glasses on crookedly, just to be different, what would happen? The person listening to me might find it impossible to look at me. I could say, "Please don't think about my glasses. Think about the things that are right about me and just ignore my crooked glasses." That would be really hard for the other person to do. There is something about us that makes us want to say, "Would you please put those things on straight?" What is the part that's got to look for flaws and try to correct them?

When I was young, our family raised chickens. I noticed that if one of the chickens had some kind of flaw, the others would peck away at it until it died. If we wanted to save its life, we had to isolate it from the other hens. Even if one of them had only a few feathers missing and just a little bit of raw skin showing, the other chickens would attack it all day long, and the next day, and keep at it until the imperfect chicken died. Is this very different from what humans do to each other?

Sometimes we feel that we can't let people get away with their imperfections, as if being critical helps the situation. Are we somehow maintaining integrity in the world by being critical?

Recently I was at an art show. As I walked around, looking at the paintings, I was criticizing them in my head. Then I felt someone standing near me. For some reason, I began to suspect that this was the artist. She was! Finally, she spoke and said, "Well, what do you think? Any criticisms?"

I could feel an instant shift in my head. It was easy to be critical. It is very challenging to make helpful comments. My first critical thoughts were coming out of the basement, but I couldn't stand next to the artist and just say, "Why don't you try something else, like golf or knitting?" I couldn't say, "The painting is all wrong, I wish you hadn't framed it." I had to come from a higher place in myself. Saying something both true and helpful takes effort and attention. It is very easy to criticize. There's nothing to it. But that *easy* criticism is usually ill-informed and destructive. If we really understood what something was like for the other person, we wouldn't be so quick to judge.

So I looked at her painting very carefully and came up with some suggestions as to how it might be improved. About an hour later, she returned to the gallery with another painting, and said, "Look, your comments were very helpful. Could you give some suggestions about this painting? I want to enter it into our annual show." Again, I had to give thoughtful and helpful comments.

Months later I went to the annual show, and there was her painting! As I was looking at it, I again felt someone standing beside me. I turned and looked. It was the artist! She thanked me for my comments. We smiled and admired the painting together. She had made many improvements, including ones I had suggested.

In the Sermon on the Mount, the Lord says, "Stop judging, so that you won't be judged. . . . Why are you looking at the wood sliver in your sibling's eye but not noticing the load-bearing beam in your own eye?"

A beam is a huge piece of wood, large enough to support a ceiling or roof. Our own mistakes and shortcomings are like this tremendous log, or beam. If we have not learned to see ourselves and deal with our own defects, how can we pick out a tiny speck or mote in our brother's eye?

HELPFUL CRITICISM?

A person who has done a lot of spiritual work might be in a position to help someone else. Anyone who has done honest and constructive self-criticism could possibly be in a position in which to help someone else by offering the right kind of criticism. I think we can safely assume that, for most of us, that day has not yet come.

There is a place for genuine criticism, but it must come out of love. Negative criticism comes out of the basement, and it is given not to improve the other person, but to make ourselves feel superior. When we criticize, we are looking down on someone else as if we had just elevated ourselves above him or her.

In Genesis 9: 20–27, we read about Noah's getting drunk and lying naked in his tent. He had three sons, Shem, Ham and Japheth. Ham went into the tent, saw his father drunk and naked, and went to tell his brothers. He might have thought that they would be amused. Instead, they put a blanket over their shoulders and walked backward so that they could cover their father without seeing him in that condition. That was a very loving and forgiving thing to do.

If you look at others from an angelic point of view, very lovingly, you will notice the good things, not the bad ones. If you see something bad, you will put the best possible interpretation on it. If you act out of the basement or the lower self, you will focus on the negative and put the worst possible interpretation on anything good. That's the difference between those two approaches.

Imagine that you saw someone go into another person's house, drag them into the alley, tie them up, and beat them mercilessly. Imagine that the person was absolutely unable to fight back. Wouldn't you be horrified? You would be especially outraged because the victim had no way to defend himself. Isn't that what we do with other people in our heads? We think bad thoughts about them. We take them down the alley and beat them up in our thoughts, and they don't even know it's happening. How can they defend themselves?

Look at criticism in your life. You might take one day to observe your critical nature, what you say or think. Then, the next day, you could try to let go of all criticism of yourself or others. This involves, first of all, observing your critical nature in action, and then seeing if you can go through a day without critical thoughts.

THE FOURTH TASK

Observe your criticisms (those you speak and those you think) for a whole day and record them in your journal. Then, once you have noticed your pattern of critical thoughts, go for a day without internal or external criticism. Notice what happens and record this in your journal as well.

REPORTING ON THE TASK

Janet: Since I was not here last week, I asked another member about what the task was, and she told me. I didn't quite understand it, but I was aware that there is one person that most of my negative things are about. But mostly, this week, I was finding positive things about him. So maybe, at another level, I really *was* working at it, although I wasn't doing it consciously.

Darren: I was driving on Fourth Avenue, and there was a car parked at an angle. And I said, "That is the *worst* parking job I've ever seen in my life." I swerved around it, and I realized that was a really severe thing to say, "the worst." On that same trip, I pulled up to a traffic light, and the light turned red, and a person drove through. I was surprised I did this, but I made a gesture, "Thumbs down to that." I was in the left-hand turn lane, I go, it turns yellow-red, and I run the light! I thought: "Oh my goodness, I just did the exact same thing! Duh!" And I realized, "Maybe she was late, maybe she had to go somewhere." I wasn't being at all compassionate.

In another instance, I was just so intensely critical about some e-mail. I was thinking, "I wrote so-and-so, and I see the date of the last time they wrote me. It's been thirty days. No, that's an exaggeration; it's actually been twenty-one or something." When I saw the date, it really made me so mad. It's like, "What is this person's problem? They can't just get on the computer and write me a note?" I get so upset about it, and I think about it and just play it over and over in my mind. And I'll even say, "Come on, man. Write me!" The person doesn't write me, and I start thinking these awful critical thoughts about them.

The task was helpful, because I started thinking, "Oh yeah, I know that this thing has happened over and over." I'll say, "You've not written me; why didn't you write me?" And they'll write back and say something awful had happened or something. And I'm like, "Oooh." I was really irate on the e-mail thing, and then I'm so sorry.

So this time instead of writing them, I was just like, "Okay, I'm just going to trust and give this person the benefit of the doubt."

I'm trying to not be so critical of that, because I see that it's my problem and it's not their problem. My criticism is my own defect.

Stewart: A friend went away on a trip and she brought over her dog for us to keep. That dog and I just don't get along at all. It barks, and the sound is so sharp it hurts my ears. Like a cat, it wants to go in and out and in and out, and it can't open the door itself. Just drives me nuts. It takes the food out of my daughter's hand and scratches her hand when she's trying to eat.

While I was cleaning, I was thinking, "You know, this dog goes to the bathroom all over the yard." And so I spent the whole rest of the week being critical of this dog. And finally tonight, I thought, "Maybe the dog's just bored." And so I took the dog on a walk with my daughter around the neighborhood. It's really annoying, you know. When a car's coming down the street, it pulls toward the car like it wants to be run over. But then I thought, "This poor dog; it's lonely. Its only master is away." This is probably the hardest task for me because I find myself justifying over and over again. I observe that I'm being critical, and then I think to myself, "But it's true! It *is* being annoying! This is a valid emotion, this is a valid criticism."

Elly: I actually surprised myself. It wasn't quite as hard as I thought it was going to be, although I was conscious of it all day, every day. I just observed how critical I was, and there are some pretty harsh things to look at. And then, the rest of the week I really tried to make a heartfelt effort. On Thursday, a coworker said to me what some people have said to me in the past that drives me nuts: "You know, you're pretty, but you'd be prettier if you smiled more." And I just hate that so much. I just want to be violent. So I just breathed, because I just found myself internalizing it, and then experiencing the hurt. "Okay, that feels like rejection." And I started to just rip them apart in my head. I knew it could turn into something really vicious, and then I just decided I wasn't going to let it. So I counted to ten, three times, and then it was fine.

Klara: I sort of focused in on the part that said, "Try one day not criticizing." So that's exactly what I did. I committed one day and didn't try and go beyond that. I did feel better on that day. I wouldn't say that I was totally successful at not criticizing, but I noticed that just focusing on that, and trying not to criticize, just made me feel a lot better inside.

Late in the week, I realized that I'd made sort of a lame effort at the whole thing. And suddenly an image of this movie that I'd seen about ten years ago came popping into my head, almost like this red-hot poker or something. There's no words in the whole movie; it's just music and people. It's sort of about mankind, and life. There're these people in South America, working in this mine, and they're just trudging up and down this muddy slope, and it's all they do, all day long. It's like ten hours, and it's all wet and grimy and smelly. I thought, "Life seems like that sometimes." I try to overcome these negative thoughts and criticisms, but sometimes it just feels like I'm trudging up this muddy slope day in, day out. And I sleep for six or eight hours, and I get up and do it again. That's how these people live their lives. And I thought, "Come on, your life's not *that* bad!" But then I thought, "Well, I guess that would be my vision of hell, in a way—just the same thing over and over."

That's what these thoughts are like, these negative thoughts and these criticisms. It's like trudging up a hill, same thing day in, day out, never really changes, the same negative thoughts, the same criticisms. It's burdensome like that, where you're going over the same ground over and over and over.

So I do feel like, here we are at Task Four, and I feel somewhat of a cumulative effect. There is a certain burden being lifted off gradually as I do these tasks, even if I don't do them as well as I think I should. It feels like, somehow, I'm making a little bit of progress.

Angus: When I started doing this task, I actually was way less critical than I ever am in a normal state of mind. It's a total psychological defense, you know. It's like, if you know you're going to have to look for these negatives, then you have less of them.

Almost every criticism I have is either a judgment of me or someone else. When I don't criticize them, it makes me give them the benefit of the doubt. Because if I don't criticize people, it makes me think of them in a different light. They might be a lot nicer, which they usually are.

Marie: I was caught in this traffic jam, and I was totally into the task, just peacefully breathing in and out. The woman in front of me got into the center lane, and then the light changed so she was kind of stuck in there. She was frantic and feeling like everyone was yelling at her. She seemed kind of angry about it, like, "Well, I couldn't help it!" So then she moved on, and then the light turned green and I went on. It turned out that the reason there was a traffic jam was there was a woman just lying down in the middle of the road. And I thought, "Wow, that really puts perspective on the situation! Who knows what's wrong with her?" So I felt like that was a good reminder for me to hold back the criticism, because there might be reasons for someone's actions.

But the people that I love the most were where my criticism came up, and it was really strong. For three days, four days, I could observe myself being critical of my husband. And I was like, "Oh, you're being critical!" But I couldn't let go of it. I just seemed really powerless and stuck in this criticism. And so then, after those four days of intense criticism, I started thinking about it. Why was I so critical? And I realized that there was this fear in me, that everything is so good, and that if I wasn't critical, I would have to be loving. And my lower self didn't want to be loving, because then I'd be vulnerable. And once I observed that, I could let go and then be a loving person.

Someone said to me, "Things in your life come from one of two places. There's either unconditional love or self-centered love." I could really see that I was coming from self-centered love and a fear of not being loved. If I'm afraid that someone's not going to love me, then I'm going to criticize them, so that I kind of have this armor on myself. And then letting go of that armor is really scary, but it's also so wonderful. I think that's why my weekend has been so great, because I was able to let go of all that stuff for a while.

Nicole: I made a list. I started writing down the stuff that I was criticizing. It was pretty bad. A lot of criticism was for the people I work for. I babysit for a family, and pretty much everything they do I criticized: the way they're raising their kids, their hobbies, what they eat, just about everything. And then there are ex-boyfriends, but I'm not going to get into that, but that was a pretty long list too. Shallow people, materialistic people, yuppie moms, eighties' hair, people's clothes. I was just really bad! I don't know if I'm bored or what—I have all this time to criticize people. I tried to observe for a couple of days, and then try to give up for a couple of days. I don't know if it was because I was giving up, but I had some really amazing days, and I don't know if it was because I was trying to, or if it was just a coincidence. But I was feeling really open and a lot more loving, so that was good.

Greg: I chose a day for this project, just to see how it would go. It was a wonderful day. And it's hard to know whether I chose the day because I thought I might be less disposed to be critical that day. I was in a very good place and feel as if I've got lots of that good elasticity and ability to react to things. But, for whatever reason, it was Wednesday, and it was just a glorious day, just in terms of feeling very focused and energetic, and feeling very capable of fending off that impulse to criticize.

What I discovered is that there were two different ways in which the criticism or tendency to criticize would arise. I would think of someone who is part of my orbit, and that maybe in conjuring that person, I might attach to them things that I viewed as something I wanted to criticize. Then there was another kind of impulse to criticize; it was almost more of a reactive thing, where I'd be presented with circumstances and then have a choice of how I was going to react to them, or whether I was going to react to them at all. So that was kind of interesting, just to realize whether it's an individual who you know or something that you're close to that sparks a critical impulse.

The really important thing is that I want to have them on my mind, and then I can take that wanting to have them on my mind and move it in a very different and very positive direction. It was really kind of great, feeling the sense of distance from oneself and watching these opportunities present themselves. It was really interesting to see that it was elasticity and ability to react that seemed to create fertile ground to start going around through my day looking for fights to pick. And so it was interesting, I found that the more resources that I had, the more possible it was to look at the world with kind of equanimity and goodwill, and not be inclined to criticize.

Keri: I just had in mind something that I think you said, about how you can always look at the negative in someone that you love if you want to. You can always find something. I sort of realized that, with a couple of key people in my life, I had fallen into a negative place, and taking time to appreciate them really helped get me out of there. I was more into seeing all the positive things, and that was good.

Bob: I worked this task a little differently. When I started to observe my criticism, I found that I was most critical of myself. I couldn't count the number of times that I said, "Bob, you dummy, you!" both out loud and to myself.

I don't know why I expect myself to be perfect in all that I do. I'm just human, but I really get down on myself when I do something as simple a making a typographical error at my keyboard. Even when I play sports for recreation, I constantly talk to myself in critical and negative ways: "Hit the ball, dummy. Move your feet, you lazy bum. Learn to play or give up the game, you idiot!"

I don't know if everyone is so critical of themselves, but I made a real effort to stop this self-criticism for one whole day. I feel better about myself.

Frank: I decided to start the task as soon as I'd left here. I was driving along, and the person in the car in front of me threw a cigarette butt out of the window. My critical self just thinks that's one of the worst things you can do. And then I went to a movie with a friend, and the friend just hated this movie. So I found myself shifting from being critical of the movie to being critical of my friend for being critical of the movie. It was such a relief to just say, "Okay, now I'm going to have a day without criticism." And I noticed it was impossible; but when the thoughts came, I just did not let them hang around too long. Still, they came very fast. I don't think there's any way to prevent critical thoughts from coming in. There were some tough situations where I was talking with people that my lower self could have made a big case about how wrong they were. But I just let go and wasn't approving of them; I was just accepting the fact they're imperfect. I'm imperfect. It's no big deal. It made for much more positive relationships.

I'm in contact with someone who is *very* negative almost on a daily basis, and virtually every word that comes out of his mouth is very critical. And then, in my head, I find myself being viciously critical for him being so critical.

It's a daily challenge not to be critical of him because he's critical. It's just the way the lower self operates. It automatically latches onto anything in order to separate us from positive thoughts and emotions.

When I am critical of someone else, there is a barrier between us. Part of what the lower self does is put up barriers between all of us. The lower self makes it hard for us to love each other.

Session Leader: Suppose you have a person who has these great, thick, dark green glasses, so when they look at you, they see a green person. If we took it personally, would they see us as green? They're still going to see us as green. They can't help seeing us as green because they have these glasses on.

Again, the lower self wants to make a case out of this. *It* wants to get upset about it instead of just observing. That is the way people who wear dark green glasses see you—as green. It has nothing to do with you; it's just the way you appear to them. But what is important is that you notice what color *your* glasses are.

TASK 5

Applying the Golden Rule

Everything you want people to do for you, keep doing likewise for them. For this is the law and the prophets.
                                            Matthew 7:12–20

You must love your neighbor as yourself.
                                            Leviticus 19:18

WE KNOW THAT WE SHOULD love one another, but it is not easy to love on command. All kinds of barriers get in the way. The people we are supposed to love can be decidedly unlovable at times. They can have all sorts of problems and character defects. They can behave in ways that make it very hard for us to love them.

When we look at our neighbor, what do we notice? We see a basement full of horrible beasts, and we think, "If it wasn't for those beasts, I could love that person." It is hard to ignore errors. We do not deal well with imperfections. We tend to focus on the flaws and shortcomings of other people.

What part of us is seeing the faults in others? Is it our higher self? Isn't it more likely to be our beasts that look at other people's beasts and think how terrible *those* beasts are.

If we can get into the higher level of being, where divine love flows through to others, we can have a wonderful feeling of acceptance and love. We do not need to focus on people's errors, perversions, or mistakes. It is only when we are acting out of our lower selves that we are harshly critical and intolerant.

It is the nature of our lower selves to find fault, although the faults inside others may be nothing compared to the faults inside us. Sometimes we suppose that other people look at us benignly and think we are wonderful. They have no difficulty loving us. *We* are the ones who have a problem loving them. "Why are they making it so hard to for me to love them?," we wonder.

How can we change this pattern? How can we break away from this illusion? One way is to put ourselves into another person's position. If you could get inside another person and live her life even for a short time, wouldn't you have an entirely new way of interpreting her behavior? You would be seeing that person from the position of her real life, instead of from what you imagine you would do in her situation. Since we do not live inside other people, however, our judgments are distorted and false.

To put ourselves in the other person's position, we have to rise to a higher level in ourselves. From that level, we can see the other person with greater sympathy.

We often have a mistaken idea about people, that if they were perfect, we would love them. When we criticize others, it is as if we say, "I couldn't possibly like him because he has so many faults." That, of course, is a lie. How do you think you would feel toward someone you thought was perfect? Wouldn't you be ter-

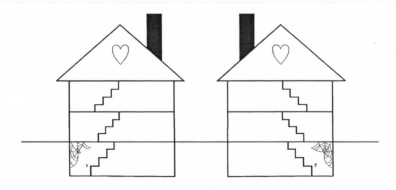

The beasts in the other guy's basement

ribly intimidated by him? Wouldn't you find that you couldn't stand him?

We imagine that other people's imperfections make it hard for us to love them, but have you ever had someone tell you in an honest and straightforward way, the realities of his or her life? Have you ever listened to the point where you started to feel their joy and their pain as if it were your own? If so, didn't you find your love toward them *increasing*? I have been in that situation many times, and in every case, I felt more love for the people who were sharing with me. Other people do not have to be perfect to be lovable.

In our normal lives, we hardly ever see people on a deep level. When they do share themselves, with all the realities of their imperfections and problems, they might expect to be rejected. Instead, they may receive an outpouring of love. In this situation, we rise above any petty criticisms and get more to the essence of a person. We see others from the point of view of their higher selves, not of their basements. We don't notice the cracks on the wall, the tottering chimney, or their unruly beasts. We look past all their flaws, and we start to tune in to their better qualities. When this happens, we feel love.

Think of people you know whom you do not like. How do you remember that you do not like them? Doesn't it take effort to keep reminding yourself, "I don't like this person"? To do this, you have to recall why it is you don't like them. Your mind will have to dig up some negative event in the past if you are to keep an attitude of dislike.

Why not put a similar effort into remembering that you *love* them? Why not put effort and attention into lowering the barriers and really coming to see the other person in a more understanding way?

THE GOLDEN RULE

The Golden Rule is *not* "Do unto others as others do to you" but "Do unto others as you would *wish* others to do unto you." And wouldn't you like other people to regard you with compassion for your problems and blemishes?

Think of someone that you have difficulty getting along with. That difficulty could be large or small. Now put yourself in that person's shoes. Take on that person's life for a few moments. If you like, fill out the form at the end of this section. Fill out the form as if you were that person. From that person's point of view, write some biographical details about the person and some facts about his or her life: What is his age? What is she doing right now? What has he experienced in the past? What is she dealing with now? This can be fairly brief, and it is only for your own reference; no one else is going to see your writing. It is just a way for you to get the picture of that other person's life.

Then write about some challenges that you—as that person— are up against. In other words, you might write: "I am Freda. I was born in 1946. I have been married and divorced. I have been alienated from my children. I have had a difficult time making ends meet. My job is not very interesting and does not pay well."

It might help to assume the other person's typical body position. Maybe the person you are thinking of always sits bent over with eyes downcast. Try sitting that way, just to help you get inside the person and begin to feel his or her life as if it were your own.

Once you have completed that task, notice whether you have a different sense of the other person and your relationship. When I have done this task, I have found that people who I thought were giving me problems were really getting many more problems from me than I was getting from them.

The task this week is to use effort and attention to get out of your critical attitude toward someone else and get into a more positive one. You can do this for a single individual, or you could apply it to a variety of people that you are having difficulties with. The task involves two steps:

1. Put yourself into the other person's shoes.
2. Make an effort to dwell on something positive about that person, rather than something negative.

THE FIFTH TASK

When you have a negative thought about another person, use effort and attention to put yourself in his or her shoes. Find one positive and true thought about the same person. Do this whenever fresh negative thoughts arise.

TASK EXERCISE: APPLYING THE GOLDEN RULE

Think of a person that you have some difficulty with. Imagine that you are that person. While role-playing as that person, write the following:

(1) Information about myself—biographical details, martial status, job information, health, and so on: _____

_____

_____

(2) Some of the challenges I face in life: _____

_____

_____

(3) How I see myself: _____

_____

_____

(4) How I see the person who is role-playing me: _____

_____

_____

REPORTING ON THE TASK

Darren: This has been a truly trying week for me. I wrote down fifty-nine names of people I resent, which is a form of criticism, obviously. And then I wrote down why I resent them. And then

I wrote down what it is in me that I feel they threaten, whether it is my self-esteem or pride or whatever. Then I wrote down where I had been selfish, inconsiderate, self-seeking, and afraid. It was truly humbling to see what I had done and where I had been selfish. It just released any negativity I felt for them, and I felt more compassion. Taking that resentment away gave space for God to come in, I guess. And see, I'm really embarrassed. I would think of someone who I had been so annoyed at, and realized I had done the same thing. So it was very humbling in that way.

I know how many people I resent, why I resent them, and it is wonderful—it really is—to see that I'm pretty much addicted to resentment. And now there's hope.

Janet: When I had a negative thought about another person, I didn't automatically switch it. Well, I tried with my little brother, who called this week. It was the first time that we had spoken some truth about situations in our family. It was out in the air, and it felt so good, but it was negative. I guess that's why I said, "Well, I don't mean to bring you down," because I had called him about something else. But it was just so refreshing. He'd laugh. He'd switch to something else and talk, just bringing out this stuff. I had buried this for years, and I told him, "This is better for me than the best therapy. Just to hear someone speak some truth about this," even though it was negative and I didn't switch it to positive things.

Stewart: I try to do the yoga sun salutation in the morning, and a morning prayer. This morning I woke up a little bit later, and my daughters were already up. I tried to squeeze in the sun salutation, and they kept crawling under me as I was wanting to go down. They thought I was a tent, and they were laughing and poking my stomach. Then they would try to jump through, and they would get bonked, and I would definitely start to resent them, thinking, "That was your own fault, that my knee bonked you on the side of the head."

I tried to put myself in their shoes, and I thought, "You know, they really just want to play with their dad, and he's doing this weird exercise thing, and why aren't they paying any attention to me?" So then, finally, I said, "I've just got to finish this last part or I'm going to be really grumpy the rest of the morning." They wouldn't leave me alone, so then I went and got them these pots and pans and chopsticks and said, "Let's have a drum thing." Because they always enjoy if I start a drum, set up a kit in the kitchen and start to play. And they were banging away, and I sat down to do the meditation, and I was thinking, "That was really dumb!" I heard, *Bang bang bang—clang clang clang—crash, ow!* I really worked hard to become unattached; I was working on this non-attachment mantra.

I was deep in this meditation, and all of a sudden they started throwing water on me. They had these cups, and they were walking around sort of sprinkling water on me. I was so deeply in this non-attachment mantra thing that I thought, "Wow, I can feel it on my skin. It's very cold." The morning was about fifty degrees, and I thought, "Boy, it's chilly, but I'm not attached to any parts of my body; it doesn't bother me." Then one of my daughters slipped in the water and fell, and I could hear her crying. And I thought, "This isn't a very good exercise, because I'm so unattached that I'm not jumping up to help her." So then I put myself in her shoes and I thought, "Boy, it would be really sad if you hurt yourself and your dad was just sitting there completely still." So I ended the meditation there.

Keri: Today there was a woman next to me, and she was talking to another secretary while I was working. They were talking about the blues festival and how there were women smoking and holding their babies. They were just talking about the pretty horrible stuff that our society has come to, and I found myself being a little critical, like, "You shouldn't dwell on that," or whatever. And then I remembered the task, and I thought of the good side of that, which is that they are aware of the fact that it isn't healthy. They're both parents, so they're really in touch with the fact that it's not a good idea to smoke with your babies right there.

Angus: On Saturday, I thought, "Finally, I have nothing to do." I was in a pretty calm state of mind, and so I had thought of a bunch of things I would like to do that night that I never do, because I don't have time. So I had all these things lined up, and I was in a pretty good mood about it. I just had to wash the dishes first. So that was going all right, and I didn't mind doing it, but then I found myself having a conversation and I realized I was not in a good mood anymore. Like I was not happy about having this night free to myself. So I tried to go back and find out where I got off track, and I found a specific spot. I was thinking of doing something musical, like writing something or recording something, but in the back of my head I had this little negative conversation, "Oh, it's probably not going to work out the way you think, or you'll get frustrated or angry." And I didn't pay that much attention to it when it happened, but it totally ruined my mood for about ten minutes, until I went back to it. It was like, "Okay, okay, I have to forget about that thought." So I didn't do too well with the task. I guess sometimes I feel like I don't do the task specifically, but it provokes a lot of things in my life that are related to the task.

Session Leader: I want to comment on that critical frame of mind. We have this thought that the reason we need to criticize people is to make them better, but what we're doing is making ourselves worse. And just observing how horrible our own state can be when we dwell in criticism is part of the self-observation thing, to just notice that. The reason for giving up criticism isn't to approve of everybody else, but to free ourselves for a more positive life. And we have all these reasons that lock us into something that's really self-destructive. "The reason I'm critical is that these people are nerds." No, the reason I'm critical is that my lower self likes that kind of stuff; it eats that kind of stuff. I can let go of that, and I'll actually enjoy life more.

Klara: I felt like I did the "Do Unto Others" task sort of in the normal course of my existence. I mean, I often do put myself in the other person's shoes and think about how they would feel about my thoughts or my actions toward them. But I couldn't really go in-depth like the exercise wanted you to. I just found other ways to be distracted, so I feel like I definitely need to do that task. So I'm going to try it again. Maybe I'll discover what the resistance is. That's just a really hard thing for me to do, especially for a couple of people that I have long-term historical battles with. I've sort of got my rote "put myself in their shoes," like, "Well, I know that this person has self-esteem problems," or "I know that this is a struggle for her." But I've been saying that for ten or twenty years or whatever, so it's not getting on to the next level of really trying to put yourself in their shoes.

Nicole: The task worked well in relation to a couple of people. There's this guy at school who works at one of those snack-vending things. He drives me crazy. I don't know what it is. He just talks and talks and talks when you just want to buy something, and he's making all these comments. He just bugs me. So that was the first person I worked on. I just tried to think that he was really friendly, and he's always telling people to have a good day, just talking a lot. So, actually, I felt a little bit better about him—didn't want to strangle him.

Then I saw my old roommate riding his bike, and he also drove me crazy. He was riding his bike, and I was driving, and I saw him. So I came up with some good things about him, and I didn't feel nearly as annoyed with him, so that was good. I'm also working some things out with a friend back home that I talked about before. It's been going on for about a year. I've been really putting a lot of effort into seeing things from her side, and it's neat. I feel like there's some reconciliation going on. I'm flying home on Wednesday to go to her wedding. It's been really crazy, but it's finally getting worked out.

Greg: I didn't work as hard or as consciously on the task as I should have. I think it is a task that requires a lot of conscious effort. I found that when I was focused on it, I would tend to become aware of some quality in a person that is irritating. But instead of really going to the effort of engaging why it is and walking in their shoes, I would retreat to that sort of fairly generic tolerance: "Well, I guess that's okay."

That doesn't do it, really, does it? All I'm doing is engaging in an exercise of tolerance or letting it not bug me, as opposed to trying to engage in the empathetic task of understanding what may be happening. So I did not fully engage the task, and I guess I'd like to make it more of a conscious effort this week.

Frank: There's a person who has been in the habit of phoning me, and some of the conversations have been long and difficult for me to handle. And this person phoned me this week, and I just assumed this was going to be a long, difficult conversation, but then I thought, "Better do the task." And it turned out it was a very positive conversation, and it was very short, and the person was asking for me to pray for her. Then I began to see how she's really working on making some major changes and improvements in her life. That was neat. So what I had to do was let go of the history of all these other phone calls, and just accept this phone call the way it was, instead of remembering all the other stuff.

I had a similar one with another person. I have some opinions about how she should run her life, and most of what I know about this woman is secondhand, not firsthand. Someone else tells me about her, and so I'm developing this fictional character in my head, and I decided that I should let go of that fictional person and just think of something true and positive. The person is very loving, and she really cares a lot. Sure, she's dealing with enormous problems; there's no question about that. But the interesting thing was, tonight when I came home, there was a gift from this person, out of the clear blue sky. So my life really is better when I let go of that stuff, especially let go of memories about people. Just take them the way they are today.

Leslie: Criticism and resentments have really been alive for me this week, and I tried to turn around some really tough ones. I moved from out of state to here, and I left a lot of things behind. I rented my house to somebody, furnished, and left a lot of my things in the house. I'm having just loads of resentment towards my tenant for not taking care of my things right, or telling me she has to throw out this or that because it's hideous. "Wait a minute, that's mine, I shopped for that, I bought that! You can tell somebody else it's hideous."

I've been trying to turn that around and realize that person is there, taking care of my things, and it's not perfect, but she's really trying hard. So I just had to keep trying to turn it around, because it's partly criticism of her and it's partly my own attachment to my things that she's got there. I try to also notice that, as we've had these conversations about it, she is changing.

One other theme that comes up in all of them is that my most vicious criticisms are reserved for myself. Any time that I'm criticizing somebody else, it has partly to do with not really appreciating myself. So if she calls my things hideous, right away I just go into this whole shame thing. There are a number of other relationship things where it's really my viciousness toward myself that's at issue. And I'm sure that this task would work just as well to have it be just focused on yourself. Maybe I'll think about myself: "When I start being really critical of myself, try to stop and think of one good thing about myself."

Noomay: The criticism for me was really hard, to be aware of what I was doing. I really was kind of scatter-brained with, "Okay, how can I remember this each day?" I was just glad to get to putting myself in other people's shoes, because it connected me more to being aware of when I was actually being critical. Because my critical mind would say, "Oh, what was that? What is being critical? Is this critical? Is that?" And then I went back to, "Oh, just do it when negative emotions come up with another person." So the task was kind of hard for me to focus on.

But I really think I needed to keep on with putting myself in others' shoes. When I've been home on my trip, it's been a good help in keeping me from going back into old patterns, especially around family. I've noticed, within a relationship, that I have so many preconceived ideas, and didn't know why I was judging but felt that judgment within myself. "Why do they treat me this way?"

So much pain is involved with that, and I just used the task. I was like, "Okay, well, let's go back to the task, and I have to put myself in this person's shoes."

I got myself there to a certain point and thought, "Okay, I did it." Then I realized that I hadn't really, and then I was like, "Okay, I have to let go of this, because it's very painful and involves so much." I pushed it to a certain point and really let go, and I just fell apart. I hadn't realized how much I needed to let go as a part of putting myself in the other person's shoes. I had seen how I had kept that distance between us, so that felt really good, "Okay, this is what it was about." It felt healing afterward.

Klara: I really did try the task of putting myself in the other person's shoes; that's what I found to be difficult. There are two people in my life in particular that I have long-standing resentments and judgments about. I feel it would be really helpful if I could put myself in their shoes, but I can't do it yet. I tried, and I guess what I realized is that, in a sense, I *have* been doing it for a long time, trying to put myself in their shoes, and the fact is that the reason I can't do it is because I think that both of these people are coming from some paranoid and irrational thoughts and feelings about life.

It's really difficult for me to put myself in that place, for me to explore how someone gets to a point of having such paranoid and irrational fears. I'm sure to them they're not paranoid or irrational, but I can't get there. I can't understand how someone gets to the point of acting and behaving based on these kinds of thoughts and feelings that end up really injuring other people.

So I feel the injury, I feel hurt, and I can't figure how these people got to that place. I'm still willing to work on it, and I think that I will go back to this task, because I think it's possible to see somehow, "Well, okay, this person has this irrational fear, because they feel insecure, or they don't feel loved, or their life didn't turn out the way they wanted it to." I think I can maybe get there, but it's really difficult. I just can't understand.

Session Leader: It sounds as if it feels that it's about them. But it's really about *you*; it has nothing to do with them.

Klara: Yeah. It was interesting that this one person in particular came up in connection with my work on the book *The Artist's Way*. In my conscious daily life, this one person really isn't affecting me that much, but it's somebody important in my life, or in my past. But I've been having these incredible dreams, where I'm so angry! This last dream I had, I was physically pummeling this person. I wake up, and it's sort of laughable because I'm like, "What is going on?" I have no conscious awareness of anything current that I'm angry about, but I think it's in connection with doing some of this work, and trying to put myself in other people's shoes. And working on some creativity things. I would like to get to the bottom of that.

Session Leader: I'd like to just remind you of something that I said at the beginning of the course. This course is about handling your internal reactions, and it's not a course on how to handle interpersonal relations.

I'd love to get into some suggestions about what to do with other people, but that diverts me from the real point of the course—how do you handle your internal state? How do you keep peaceful and loving and happy and positive in the face of rude people? I think we all have to deal with that. You eventually get to the point where it really doesn't matter what the person does. You stay in heaven. You don't let them get you out of that. And once you tell yourself, "He's doing the best he can," the lower self gets somewhat frustrated. It wants to criticize. It says, "But, but, but." You must say, "He's doing the best he can!" The lower self's like a mongrel dog that likes to bite people.

TASK 6

Taming the Wild Elephant

Be still and know that I am God.

Psalm 46:10

After he had gotten up, he reprimanded the wind and said to the sea, "Be still, be quiet."And the wind died down, and there was a great calm.

Mark 4:39

THIS TASK RELATES to the challenge of dealing with strong negative emotions. We can go for a day or a week without huge upsets. Then there are times when the emotions are so powerful that they just take over. They come over us like a steamroller, and we can't do anything about it.

Crises in life bring up emotions that are extremely difficult to handle—rage, depression, or fear. Sometimes, when these powerful emotions take over, they are difficult to control. We can learn something about controlling negative emotions from the manner in which wild elephants are trained in India.

Elephants are used to move telephone poles and to do other jobs. When another elephant is needed, a wild one must be taken from the jungle. Then it must be tamed and trained.

How do you tame a wild elephant? You don't just walk up to an elephant and say, "Nice elephant, go over and pick up that log." It's no use getting on the elephant's back and riding it as if you were breaking in a horse.

This is what elephant trainers do: they get two tame elephants that have been working together for a long time and put one on each side of the wild elephant. These two elephants go about their business, picking up logs and moving things. If the wild elephant gets frisky, they just sort of lean on it. After some time, the wild elephant has calmed down and learned to work like the rest of them.

What has that got to do with spiritual growth? The wild elephant in this example represents our negative emotions. As far as our emotions are concerned, the wild elephant could be something like runaway fear, uncontrollable rage, acute depression, or any emotion that is strong and out of control. It is no use trying to deal with the emotion directly. When someone is afraid, it does not help to say, "Don't be afraid." The fear will continue, and the person will get annoyed. When you say, "Don't be angry," an angry person will only get more angry. You can't talk to emotions. They don't listen.

Try talking to your own emotions, and you will see how useless that is. Talking to someone else's emotions is just as useless. A person will not stop worrying just because you tell her to.

So it seems as if there is nothing you can do, but there is. You can deal with the tame elephants. And what are the tame elephants? They represent the two areas of your life that are somewhat under your control.

One of them is your body and your body tensions. You will notice that when your emotions get out of control, your body also gets out of control. Can you imagine a person being furious without having some physical symptom? Can a violently angry person have a normal heartbeat, relaxed hands, and a face with its usual color? No. If you are angry, your body will show it. In fact, the anger cannot survive if your body is relaxed. I used to think that, if my body were tense, I couldn't do anything about it. Then I learned that if I can tense my body, I can relax it. I have some control over that. And the same is true of thoughts. I can do something to control thoughts—not totally, but at least in part.

By working on relaxing the body, you work on one of the tame elephants, and this puts pressure on the anger to relax. This is true of other emotions. People feel fear in their gut. If you can relax your stomach, it is very hard for that fear to survive.

One of the ways in which you tame the body is by noticing the tensions, maybe exaggerating them a little bit, and then relaxing. The point of tensing your muscles further is to remind yourself that you have some choice as to whether your body is tense or relaxed. You might have to do these steps repeatedly, but they will work. Since you are able to tense your muscles, you can relax your muscles. You bring that elephant alongside by taming the body.

The other elephant to bring alongside is your thoughts. You will notice that wild emotions need wild thoughts. If someone makes you angry, you get all kinds of crazy thoughts: "This person is always doing that to me. I can't stand it" or "I don't know why everyone is bugging me today. Everybody's on my back."

Wild thoughts support the wild emotions. Just as you can relax your body, so you can relax your thoughts. Emotions that are based on tensions will not long survive in a relaxed body whose mind is full of positive thoughts.You can either stop the thought and just say to your mind, "Shut up; that's not helpful," or you can replace the negative thoughts with positive ones.

The time will come when you are really tested. We read about the tragedies some people have to deal with in life. How do they get through them? We might have to deal with some rough things in our own lives as well. What will we do? When we are faced with difficult situations, it is useful to have this particular exercise available to us.

THE SIXTH TASK

When a negative emotion is active in you, first become aware of your body and any body tensions. Make them more tense and then relax. Then observe your thoughts. Stop negative thoughts and/or replace negative thoughts with positive ones. Observe any changes in your emotions.

REPORTING ON THE TASK

Angus: This one was pretty easy because of what we were saying last week about how you get tension when you drive. I commute to work, about twenty minutes. I used this a lot when I was driving, especially at stop lights. It did make me relax a lot more, and I realized that I'm almost never late for work. Occasionally I am, but I drive every day like I'm going to be, even if I'm nowhere near being late. I'm like, "Get out of my way! I gotta go to work!" I'm really hyped up. But I noticed if I relax my body, that totally changes my thoughts. It also changes my whole perception of every other driver on the road. If somebody is going slow, I'll try and think of reasons. I used to get mad because I'd get behind winter visitors all the time. But I found that if I pretend it was my grandparents driving the car, and then I would think of them and what would they feel if I was right up behind them. They'd be so mad at me, and I would be so embarrassed to be doing that to them.

I've also been thinking about getting more creative. There are just so many huge parallels between being spiritual and being creative, you know. When you get rid of negative stuff, I think it is impossible to be spiritual without also becoming creative in the process. It's impossible to have your body be relaxed and then have negative thoughts. And it's the same thing, I think, with your mind. It's impossible to have a good, spiritual state of mind and then not be creative.

Keri: There were pointless thoughts that were trying to get me. I realized that there are few areas in my life where they really get me. It's amazing how they can. For example, with creativity. If I hear in my head, "Oh you can't do this, you can't create," then I feel like there's no point to anything. It just totally encompasses everything and sums up my life in this one negative feeling. And so I'm trying to combat that and just say, "Yes, I can do it." And for some reason right now, it's working.

Nicole: I guess it was good that I didn't have to use the elephants when I was home. I thought I was going to, but actually it went really well. It's always strange going home, but this was good.

It's a long story, but there's a friend of mine from back home that I've had a problem with for the last year, and I went home for her wedding, and I did a reading. It was really good for me, because I've been feeling like I've been holding on to this need for her to talk everything out with me, and really work through things. About a month ago, I still hadn't talked to her, but I just decided I was tired of feeling like this and so I decided to buy a plane ticket anyway.

I went back and forth after that, but when I bought the ticket I felt like I was really coming from a place of love. That day was probably more emotional and more relieving than the actual trip home, because I think that was a big breakthrough. I was nervous going home and nervous to see her family and everything, but it turned out really well, and I'm glad that I went. I don't know what's going to happen with our friendship. It's kind of up in the air, but I feel much better about it.

Elly: I had a phone visit with someone, and we're going through a really difficult time. This person has a really serious eating disorder, and I found myself about thirty or forty minutes into the conversation just sort of tuning out, because this has been going on about eight years. It's taken a big toll on our friendship in a way, because at some point it feels like, "It's all you talk about, really." The eating disorder is so serious, and it's been life-threatening at a couple of different stages.

I felt guilty and tense, and I was actually sort of hoping the time would pass—hoping that I could get off the phone. I hated myself for doing that, but at the same time it almost felt like survival, because at some point, I just felt like screaming, "Why don't you just change? Why don't you just stop it?" It seems so easy to say that, but it wouldn't benefit either one of us. So when I got off the phone with her, I relaxed a little bit, remembering the tame elephants, so that helped.

Greg: It was a very interesting week, and I found that I spent most of my time pulling my card out dutifully each morning to see what meditation lay waiting for me. Kind of just ringing the changes on the words and letting them soak in, and I found that it was the one elephant I needed to have on the job. It was plenty adequate for making for a very fulfilling and focused week.

Session Leader: It strikes me, as you're talking, that when you meditate like that, you are using both elephants. You're relaxing your body and you're bringing other thoughts into your mind.

Greg: I suppose so, yes. I think that's right. As I allow myself to dwell on the sense of the words, there's really not much room for tension. One thing I did find myself thinking [about] is that old Talmudic tradition, about thinking of the Torah day and night, and how sweet it is to just dwell on this. That had never had any particular meaning for me one way or the other, but I began to say, "Well, yes, I can see how that might very well be so, that just by abiding in these words and letting them work in me, that some fairly remarkable transformations can occur." I wouldn't dream of calling any of mine remarkable, but I've sort of got an intimation of some remarkable possibilities.

Leslie: When I'm in the middle of an emotion, I have trouble remembering I have work to do around this task. A couple of times, I did remember to be conscious of it, but I'm not sure what to do with this. I found myself crying about something, and so I looked around for what was tense, and it was more like the opposite, that I couldn't find any tension. If it was maybe not such an appropriate situation for letting tears flow, I could tense up my facial muscles or my neck muscles, trying to stop it. So it was more the opposite thing I was noticing. And noticing too that at moments when my body is completely relaxed, like when I'm down on the table for an acupuncture treatment, nothing to worry about except this good treatment I'm going to get, I start to cry. I was crying because I lay down and let go, and out it came. So I don't know what to make of that one. There wasn't anything I could tense up to make the emotion more tense.

Klara: One thing that's been really different for me is that I'm almost five months pregnant, and it's a totally different experience. I notice that I'm on a real even keel. I guess that's why I dream about being angry, because during the waking day even things that would normally make me really tense or angry, my body won't go there. It just will not go there. At first, I was, "What the heck is this?" I've admitted before that I do sort of revel in these negative emotions, so at first I was thinking: "Okay, now I'm getting really, really angry. Okay, okay, I'm waiting." And it doesn't happen, and I'm disappointed. I know it sounds really terrible, but I can't reach that intensity, high or low. But I've gotten over that now; I don't feel disappointed.

I feel like I wish I could market this, whatever it is that keeps me on this even keel. I know there's things like Prozac, but this is good stuff! It's not like I don't experience any tension, but not like I'm used to, so it seems like nothing. But a few times when I have noticed feeling tense or anxious, I focused on the physical sensation. Something I notice about tension and relaxation is that, if I feel it in my neck and relax my neck, it jumps to another part of my body. That's really frustrating, because I'm relaxing, but now my head is pounding, then it's in my thighs. So it takes a while to get there, but once I am fully relaxed, I do notice that there's no negative emotion. The emotion is gone.

Darren: The only thing I really remembered about the task was the relaxation—to relax when I started getting negative. Simple things like coming up to a traffic light I always have this thing like, "Things are going well when they keep turning green. Yeah, things are going my way." And then when I'm coming up and it turns yellow, I'm like, "Oh, darn!" And I can feel it in my body; my body starts to get tense. But then I relaxed and looked around, and the funny thing is, I noticed the shift of this rushing.

There was a fire on the mountain; I guess they're purposely doing these fires. And I came to a stop where I usually would get a green, because I have these consistent paths I travel. And I looked at the smoke up there, and I was like, "Oh man, I hope it doesn't turn soon because this is really cool to watch." So suddenly my rushing was the exact opposite; I wanted to sit there as long as I could. "No, I'm just going to sit here for a while, just for the heck of it." Just sort of look around.

Stewart: I had an interesting weekend. My spouse took one of my daughters to a reunion back East, so I was with my eldest daughter, who's almost four. It was a very challenging weekend. I guess the elephant thing, the thing I was really thinking about happened this morning. I missed my morning prayer; if the girls get up before me, then I miss that chance to get in my morning meditation and prayer. So I always try to slip it in during a quiet time, which is sometimes a mistake. This morning they were playing, I made a tent for them, and they were playing in there. And then they realized that I was meditating, so they came over and started bouncing up and down on my knees. It hurt a little bit, but I was really at a great place with the breath, unattached, but then it got pretty bad. They started pulling my hair.

I thought, "Oh, I should probably try to move to a different place; I'll go outside and shift the energy out there, and they'll run around in the grass while I'm meditating." So I got up on top of this big tank that we have, and I remembered the elephants, and I thought, "Wow, I've got two tiny little wild elephants, one of either side of me!" My legs were in the lotus, and my one daughter was slapping my knee with all of her might—you know how a little kid can do that. I was really deep in this meditation, and I thought, "Wow, she's probably going to stop and I'll be able to continue." It keeps stinging, and I'm really focusing on that knee, and then she just kept slapping. Wap! Wap! And then giggling, and she kept doing it. And my other child was screaming, and I thought, "This is just the opposite of the task! Where can I get four or five trained elephants to come herd those other ones away?"

But because I stuck with the meditation, and I could feel all these feelings—my knee is turning red, and it stings, and I could feel all of those things running up and down inside of my chest. And I just stuck with the breath, and then when I came out of it, they started fighting about something. I was really able to be super-compassionate after that. I was surprised. All those feelings of anger, "Stop slapping me!" could just be there, and I was somewhere else.

Marie: I just had incredible, numerous opportunities to work on taming the wild elephant. When you gave us the task, I was already nervous about an upcoming bodywork session, where it's always very, very painful. So I was already starting to get tense about that. So the next day, when I got in the car, I was like, "I'm really tense about this thing. I know I'm going to be feeling pain." And then my immediate reaction was to go for the radio, to turn it on to escape my fear. I was like, "No, no. I'm not going to escape it; I'm just going to feel it." And immediately, I just thought, "Well, okay. Think about the elephants." I relaxed, and all of a sudden, well, I kind of got this message, "Oh, you're relaxed now. Now you can turn on the radio." And I turned on the radio, and there was this guy on the radio that was actually a friend from back home!

He was talking all about relaxation, and I was just getting so nourished from this radio program. He started talking about how important breath is, and taking deep breaths, and all these reasons. So then I started taking deep breaths, and those deep breaths got me through the whole week. Every time I started getting tense or anxious, I realized that I wasn't breathing, and I would start taking deep breaths and immediately got so much more relaxed.

That was a hard thing, and there were a lot of successes that were easy, like meeting all these old friends I hadn't seen for ten years brought up so much anxiety. Being able to breathe through that, I just felt that the task gave me so much freedom. Then, on the way home, our airplane had a problem and everyone was like, "Oh, we're never going to get home!" I could feel these thoughts coming in, like, "Oh, I'm not going to get to see husband or my child tonight." But then, "Let go, breathe, you're here with your daughter, you're able to sit here and stretch and eat pretzels." So I just felt like, "Wow, this is so freeing!" Because I saw so many people around me just trapped in these negative states, and I was very grateful for having tools to relax.

Frank: I've been having this battle with a government agency, and it tends to bring up a lot of negative emotions because there are thousands of dollars at stake. I had another phone call, and I decided, "Well, just relax." And as I was listening to the representative, I realized that he was my friend, not my enemy, and he was working with me, not against me. So changing that thinking, and just saying, "Something will work out; it's okay," it became a much calmer and more pleasant experience. But basically I've gone the week with very few times in which I've felt the need for the task. I liked that; I like having a week where I don't need to use this tool.

Bob: I didn't have a chance to use this task until yesterday evening when, during a party, it occurred to me that I would be called on to make a speech. My body began to chill and negative thoughts were beginning to come into my head. "What am I going to say? How am I going to introduce myself?"

But I just said, "I should relax." And I was able to put down a few points which I used in giving the speech. I think the relaxation and allowing my body and mind to feel at rest helped me a lot.

Session Leader: I'll give you another example of taming the wild elephant. A woman got on an airplane. The plane was about to take off, and already she was afraid the plane might crash. The passenger sitting next to her said, "I wonder if anybody listens when the stewardess tells you about the escape hatches, the oxygen, and all that kind of stuff."

He looked over at her. Her eyes were riveted to the attendant. This was her first airplane flight. She was listening to every word. She wanted to know where the exits were. She wanted to know where the flotation thing was under her seat. She wanted to know everything. She was a mess. Her emotional state showed in her physical tensions and in her wild thoughts: "I just know this plane is going to crash. My children are going to be orphans. Or maybe I will just be maimed for the rest of my life. I can't stand it. I have to get out of here."

She could have used this exercise. She could then have leaned back in her seat, let her arms relax by her side. She would have turned her mind to positive thoughts: "The plane has not even taken off. Very few of these planes crash. It is exciting to have my first plane journey. Worrying about crashing will not prevent it from happening. If something goes wrong I can start worrying then. It does not do any good to worry about that now." All of that would have eased the emotion and tamed the wild elephant.

TASK 7

Dealing with Lying

Stop your tongue from evil; your lips are not to speak deceptively.

Psalm 34:13

Remove from me the way of lying.

Psalm 119:29

SOME PARENTS ONCE APPROACHED ME with a concern about their two-year-old child. "We've noticed that our child is starting to lie," they said. "The other day we asked him if he had taken a cookie. He denied it, but had a cookie in his hand! It was a great shock. We have always told him the truth. How did he learn to lie?"

That's a good question. How *do* we learn to lie? Children certainly have motivation to lie. They learn that telling the truth can get them in trouble, and lies can save them. They also learn that they can use lies to get someone else in trouble. They discover that their parents can't read their thoughts. Lying often seems to be a very smart thing to do.

Where do the lies come from? One source is our instinct for self-preservation. If we are afraid the truth will hurt us, we will twist the truth or deny it. We also lie when we are negative. An angry person might say outrageous and false things. A depressed person might make things look worse than they are. A greedy person might tell lies to get some advantage.

A friend of mine, who for many years was a car dealer, commented on the reputation of people who sell second-hand cars. "I know people who sell used cars are liars," he told me once. "Every time someone comes in to buy a new car he lies about his old one to try to get the best dollar for it!" A few years ago another friend had a minor fender-bender. The other people walked away from the accident looking absolutely fine. Later they told her that there was nothing wrong with them, and they would not sue for damages. A few months passed, and my friend's insurance bill came through. She questioned why it was so high. The company said that the other people in the accident put in a claim for $3,000 for their physical injuries! She knew, of course, that someone was lying. What could she do? There are many cases like that where people fake accidents or claim injuries that did not take place. They lie. They manage to get their doctor to lie. It pays to lie. It's as simple as that.

Recent studies have shown that our society is riddled with this kind of distortion of the truth. It seems that many people assume that lying is a necessary part of survival and that everybody does it. In some cases, it involves money. In other cases, like the person who claims credentials he does not have or boasts of exploits he never achieved, it might seem as if lying is often a victimless crime. "What difference does it make if I exaggerate a little bit? No one gets hurt."

Lying comes from our lower self. It might seem to be harmless, but it does serious damage to credibility and trust. On a deeper level, it hurts our relationship with the truth.

I once knew a little girl who had a serious problem with lying. It had become so habitual with her that I doubt if she knew the difference anymore. It seems to have injured her ability to see the truth clearly.

Lying can take many different forms. There are the obvious lies, the ones we call boldfaced lies. This is when we say something that we know is not true. This is not the only form of lying. People in twelve-step programs come to see the danger in rationalizing or making excuses. They tell stories about all the justifications they have given in the past for their particular addiction.

"I drank because I was so lonely" says one. "I drank because there were too many people in the house" says another. "I drank because my father drank." Whatever the supposed reason, it is almost certain to be a lie, the kind of lie that makes excuses for things we know are wrong. If we want to do something we can always make up reasons for doing it, but this is just lying to ourselves.

Exaggerations are also lies. Some people get so much into the habit of stretching the truth that their friends will say, "How much shall I divide your figures by this time?" We have seen cartoons of fishermen holding their hands wide apart to describe the fish they caught. The people watching know that this is a lie.

Our self-important self wants to appear to know more than it does. There are times when we can hear ourselves holding forth on some subject that we may know very little about. Other people can goad us into this form of lying by asking questions as if they expect us to know the answer. It is hard to resist falling for this bait.

We can even say true things with the intent to deceive, like the Cold-War story about a race between a Russian and an American. The American papers reported: "There was a race between an American and a Russian, and the American won." *Pravda* reported: "There was a race involving different countries. The Russian runner came in second. The American just barely finished before the last man." While technically true, the report amounts to being a lie.

Then there are those wonderful lies by omission, like the man walking down the aisle with his bride. She notices another woman breaking into the church screaming: "That's my husband you are marrying!" He turns bright red, turns to her and said: "Didn't I tell you that I was already married?"

One of the most common forms of lying comes under the category of "white lies," things that we say because they will make the other person feel better, but we know that they are not true, like the man who told his new bride that he loved her tapioca pudding. Years later it finally came out that he hated it. "Why did you say you liked it?" she asked. "I knew you had gone to a lot of trouble to make it, and I wanted to please you" was his reply. It is inevitable that a certain amount of this kind of lying will go on in society, but there is a cost in terms of credibility. I think most of us would prefer to hear the truth.

It is generally believed that people with terminal diseases would rather know the truth than be lied to. When I was young, doctors and family would routinely hide the facts about a patient's condition if it was very serious. This might have been done to be kind. Many people are rethinking that particular version of kindness.

Another form of lying is making promises you have no intention of keeping. This is lying about the future. "Yes, I will come to your wedding." Caterers have learned to caution couples that for every one hundred people that promise to come to their wedding, only about eighty will show up.

There are probably other forms of lying. Within all of the examples above, there is the strange practice of lying to yourself. Much of the negative self-talk we have comes under the category of lying. Sometimes we tell ourselves that we are better than we are. In more cases, we put ourselves down. We need to understand these and many other forms of lying, and come to love speaking the truth to ourselves and to others.

THE SEVENTH TASK

1. Observe *It* (your lower self) lying by:
   a. saying to yourself or to another what is not true
   b. rationalizing—making excuses by lying to yourself
   c. exaggerating (externally or internally)
   d. talking with authority about something you know little or nothing about (for example, the federal budget)
   e. saying things that are true with the intention to mislead

    f. lying by omission (leaving out some vital piece of infor-
       mation)

    g. telling "nice" lies to be kind

    h. making promises you do not intend to keep.

2. When you observe the lying, stop.

REPORTING ON THE TASK

Nicole: I didn't do so well with the lying task. There were a couple of times where I noticed myself getting ready to lie in case I had do. I'm thinking about this situation where I might have to tell a story. The couple of times I remember thinking that, but I don't think I actually had to. So that was good, I guess.

Session Leader: Well, at least you have a choice. Before you observe it, you just do it. Once you observe it, you say: "Well, do I want to do this or not?" And you might still choose to do it, but at least then you'll be aware of it. You'll be working on a different level.

Keri: I noticed I really enjoyed lying, blatantly, like right in someone's eyes, planning to tell them the next second that I'm lying, you know. Just saying something outrageous, just because I just really like that. So I noticed myself doing that a few times, and even getting a bigger kick out of the fact that it was the task!

Stewart: I felt like there was one or two days during the week when I really thought about the lying. The rest of the time, I sort of had it on the back burner. My worst one is speaking with authority about subjects I know little about, just wallowing in those. Usually I would just sum up at the end of my whole thing, "And by the way, I'm speaking without authority about that," but I'd already presented it as if I was the authority, so that was sort of a weak attempt at correcting myself.

Angus: I'm not a liar, and I didn't catch myself doing a lot of it this week. Just because it seems like as soon as I would start to do something I'd stop myself. It would probably be good for me to do the task a week later than everybody else, and then I'd really be doing it; I wouldn't be pretending. But I did notice that I lied to myself a lot; that's my biggest thing, not admitting how I feel about something, or making up criticisms that are not true. That's where most of my lying comes in.

Elly: The lying was fairly painful. As Angus said, I find that I lie mostly to myself, in terms of pretending that I don't feel certain things, or if I feel really hurt, I'll make excuses and I'll stuff it. That's just denial. "No, I'm okay; no, it doesn't matter. I'm tough, and don't need anything." So I end up getting hurt by that. And then I found myself lying about a relationship that I'm in, and I've done this before—it's a really weird pattern. I don't know why, but when talking to someone about something going on in *their* relationship, it's like I have to compensate and I have to relate to them somehow, so I'll say, "Oh yeah! Well, *he* does that all the time too!" Then I realize, "Wait, that's not true! Why am I saying that?"

This week, especially, I caught myself almost every time I did that. It's sort of weird. And then I apologized to the one person, saying, "I'm really sorry, and I lied about it." And then today, there was kind of an explosion, because I was in a board meeting with some clients, and my boss is about to have a baby any second, and she was trying to change the soda machine, and there's these little things like Diet Coke and Coke that you have to refill and carry them out and everything, and I didn't want her to do that because she's can't breathe because the baby's pushing up. "Oh here, let me do that." She says, "Oh, you know how to do that?" "Oh yeah, of course!" Well, it turned out I did it wrong, and the whole thing just went everywhere. There was Coke all over me, and during the board meeting people are staring at me, and my face is turning red. And I was like, "Oh, I wish I hadn't lied." That's the ongoing task for me.

Session Leader: That's the important thing. We must observe. You can observe and choose to be nice or choose to tell a nice lie. If you observe it first at least you are choosing it and not just doing it automatically.

There is a question of strategy in dealing with other people. The spiritual work is how to deal with yourself. The key is to observe and see that you are telling "white lies." Observing what you are doing gives you a chance to make a choice to continue to do it or to do something else.

Klara: There wasn't anything that came up immediately for me, except when I lied to the leader on the hike. He said, "Is everyone happy?" and I said, "Ecstatic." I guess it was pretty obvious that I was being sarcastic because I wasn't feeling ecstatic at all. I had a miserable ride from the church to the beginning of the trail, but I confessed immediately and was absolved. So nothing really significant came up this week. I guess I just spent a lot of time thinking about lying in my life, like what are the patterns or what are my experiences.

The only thing I could really come up with as a current issue is in two different situations where I'm sort of conspiring to withhold information from certain individuals. I feel sort of justified in doing it because I'm withholding information about things that I'm doing, that I don't feel they necessarily need to know. Although, I guess the reason I'm withholding it is because I thought they would have negative reactions. So it kind of took me a while to identify the withholding as a lie. I still sort of resist it, because I feel so justified in the situation. So it wasn't until the end of the week that I realized those two situations were a form of lying.

Darren: As for lying, I actually think I did pretty well. I exaggerated here and there, but I didn't come across too many instances where I thought, "Oh, I want to lie here, and won't." It probably just happened to be circumstance, because if the situations had happened to have arisen, I would have been tempted to lie.

Noomay: I think the part that caught my attention the most was all these different forms of lying. I was lying to the Lord. I wasn't being truthful about my true self and that was just realizing that was the hardest part. I definitely didn't have a problem finding different kinds of lying once I started looking and meditating on it.

At first I was kind of like, "Was that lying?" And trying to figure it out. But then I was more like . . . , well, I just came up with a list of things. Delusion was a kind of lying that came up. Insincerity was a really big one. Again, I guess it's sort of a form of lying to myself. Just the subtle harmfulness of that, I was just kind of denying the truth, the everyday truth that's there. Like with insincerity, I would think of something I was doing, and think, "Well, why am I doing this? Whose benefit is this for?" And if it wasn't really for the Lord, it was kind of like a lie. There's a lot of these little subtle things that came up. Everywhere I read it was just like, "Wow, that's some form of lying." I just talked to myself about it, and thought, "You liar!" But then I thought, "Oh wait, but that's not really . . . I'm not" . . . instead of saying "*It* is lying." That's also sort of a lie too.

One more thing: There was a blatant lie that I told. I didn't admit to it, and I just felt really bad. I just felt the excuses coming and saw the workings of how sneaky I was. So that was the blatant thing that kept me thinking about it throughout the week. There's just too much to think about.

Greg: I used to be just a terrible liar, in terms of sugar-coating things to make unpleasant realities seem less so. And I've become a lot better about that, and like someone else mentioned, I think the very fact of concentrating on lying makes you less susceptible to doing it. But I do lie. I exaggerate the bleakness of things— that's probably one of my most characteristic lies, whether it's criticizing someone else or assessing the difficulties that are facing me. They're always presented to me as tougher than, in fact, they are.

One blatant but probably harmless lie I told this week was one of those instances where somebody ambushes you with a question, and you're not really sure that they have a right to the answer. So rather than saying something like, "Well, I'm not going to tell you the answer," or whatever, you just lie. I don't think you need to lie. I was thinking about that just this evening, that I could probably do just as well saying something that was noncommittal, or just saying, "Well, I'm not going to tell you." I was thinking about that, and I realize that I tell lies because sometimes I'm not sure that the person can be trusted with the truth—that I'm not so sure they're a good custodian of the truth. And so therefore, I won't tell the truth, but I won't admit the fact that I'm not telling the truth. I don't know what to make of that. I think I was just contemplating that reality, and realizing that maybe that's something that needs a little bit of work.

Frank: I noticed an exaggeration: trying to impress someone with how long something was, compared to if you did it the other way, how short it would be. I said, "It would only take one minute." I'm sure it would take ten, so I divided by a factor of ten, which is pretty severe. But I found, taking a group on a hike—I try to learn about plants and rocks and trails and things, and so people feed into that and they ask me these questions, and so many times I have no idea what I'm talking about. And here we were going on a hike, and I've never been on this trail before. Nobody in the group had been on the trail before, but I was still being the expert on the trail. So that was pretty sick.

One other form of lying that I noticed: I was with someone, and I was having some negative reactions to them. Then I thought, "If I was going to be truthful, I would tell them this negative stuff," but I didn't feel like that was going to work with them, so I shifted to just praying for them, trying to see something positive, so that I wouldn't have this incongruence going on: I'm with people, I'm visiting with them, I'm talking to them, and just thinking black thoughts about them. I decided to shift my thoughts, and it made for a much more pleasant time. But this is a challenging one.

Marie: I'm just a big liar. I realized that anytime I'm talking, I talk about why somebody else would be doing something, or why they're acting that way. That's totally lying since I have no idea what's going through anybody else's head. And also about the world, I really have no clue about what's going on in the world. Like even when I do listen to the media, it's all based on hearsay, because who knows whether the media know what's going on. So, I just thought I should have only talked about my experience.

But the main thing I focused on with the lying was, I remember listening to a tape and on the tape it was saying that whenever you're in a negative state, that there's a lie somewhere. And I noticed that with my daughter. One time I was putting her down for a nap, and my meal was ready for me, but I wanted to get her down first, and then I really noticed I was in a negative state about this. I was trying to be calm, and look at it, and I was saying, "You need to take a nap, because tonight's Halloween and if you're going to have fun, you need to rest." But the fact that I was in the negative state, I knew there was a lie somewhere. So then I was looking at this, and the truth was I wanted her to take a nap. It wasn't for her that she was taking a nap. I wanted her to take a nap so that I would have more fun tonight. And as soon as I was aware of that, I could let go of the whole thing and I said, "Well, get up. Who cares? If you're tired, then you'll go to sleep later." So that was really relieving.

Leslie: I found myself thinking, "Wait, am I supposed to do this whole thing in one week and have done with it?" This is a really hard one for me. The task of dealing with lying, observing when there's lying: internally, or little white lies, any kind of evasion of the truth. I think I always struggle with that. I get truly outraged when I notice somebody not being straight and truthful with me. It bothers me a lot, and I think I most don't like it when I want to be truthful about something that I feel passionate about, and I don't know how much my emotions are pushing me in one direction or another. And maybe I don't have a way to check out whether the other person really said what I think they said, or meant what I think they meant. I guess all of these tasks are things that I have to work on over and over again. This is one that I'd really like to work on more.

There was one moment when I noticed myself telling a white lie, and feeling like there was no other way to be nice in that moment than to not speak the truth. And then I just made a note of that internally, because I knew that I'd be working on this. I guess I could work for hours on what else I could have done at that moment. It was just somebody who was trying to have a conversation with me at a moment when I just didn't want to converse, and I said something dismissive, and the person said, "Do you want me to leave you alone?" And I said, "Oh no! It's all right. Really, I'm just tired," and all this stuff, when I could have said, "Yes."

Session Leader: I think we pay more dearly for nice lies than we imagine. One of the prices that we pay is that we don't believe one another. There is a huge credibility gap. After a while, the people in your life are being so nice to you, you don't believe anything they say. So there's a distance created by white lies that tends to destroy relationships.

People think that no one cares and that these little lies don't matter. But if we get into careless habits, it can really damage our own ability to tell the difference between truth and falsity. That is a great loss.

TASK 8

Living in the Present

In your eyes a thousand years are like the yesterday that just passed, and like a watch in the night. . . . Make well known to us that we should number our days, so that we may be clothed with a heart of wisdom.

Psalm 90:4,12

Don't worry about tomorrow, for tomorrow will worry about itself. Today's evil is enough for today.

Matthew 6:34

When people are in a heavenly state of love or good feeling, if they feel no impatience, they are in an angelic state suspended from time.

Emanuel Swedenborg, *Arcana Coelestia* 3827

To God, what is going to happen and what exists now are the same thing. In fact for him the whole of eternity is here and now.

Emanuel Swedenborg, *Arcana Coelestia* 2788

WHAT HAS TIME got to do with spiritual life? What is the relationship between the way we handle time and our spiritual life? The issue here is learning to live in the present.

If we do not live in the present, what is the alternative? We either live in the present, or in the past, or in the future. When do we live in the past? We do it in the present. When do we live in the future? We do it in the present.

"Not living in the present" is really describing a way of using our mental energies. There are two pitfalls for each direction that we look. When we look back, the pitfalls are thinking "it was great," or thinking "it was terrible." "It was great" can bring up dissatisfaction with the present. "It was terrible" can awaken painful memories.

When we live in the future, the one pitfall is "It's going to be great" and the other is "It's going to be terrible." "It's going to be great" can lead to dissatisfaction with the present, and "It's going to be terrible" brings up worry and anxiety. There is nothing wrong with enjoying memories of the past, or looking forward to something in the future. The problem lies in the negative emotions of regret and fear that can disturb our peace of mind in the present.

It is easy to go through life waiting for something to happen. But what does that do to the quality of our life now? We spend our lives waiting.

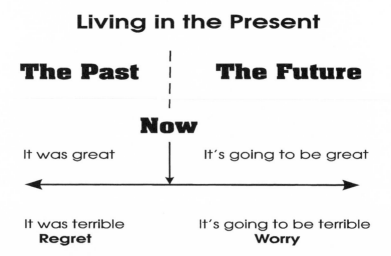

Living in the Present

The Past | **The Future**

Now

It was great | It's going to be great

It was terrible
Regret | It's going to be terrible
Worry

What is the value in remembering some past event and then feeling bad about it? What does that do to our spiritual lives? If it makes us feel worse about life, it probably comes out of the basement. It does not improve the quality of life.

I would like to illustrate this with the case of a man working on a conveyor belt. His job is to sort oranges. The oranges are coming past at great speed. Some are good and some are bad. When he sees a bad orange, he takes it off the conveyor belt and pitches it into the wastebasket. There is only a very short section of the belt where he can actually touch the oranges.

If he looks to the left, he sees the oranges that have already gone past. He can say, "Oops, I missed a rotten orange. That is terrible!" Of course, by the time he has done that, many more oranges have passed him by. If he looks to the right, he sees the oranges coming toward him, and he says, "Oops, there is a rotten orange coming toward me. This is going to be terrible!"

Again, if he is only looking at what is coming, he cannot deal with the oranges right in front of him. The only value of looking at the oranges that are about to come is that it could help him grab the rotten ones when they come within his grasp. If he's going to do his job, the only way he can operate is in the present.

WORK ON THE QUALITY OF LIFE

The only time we can work on the quality of our life is in the present. Think of the psychic energy we spend dreading or looking forward to something in the future. Think of the energy we put into regretting the past or saying "It used to be good, but it isn't anymore." This attempt to live some time other than in the present comes from the beasts in the basement. Once they get us away from the place where we are living, we end up in some kind of negative emotion.

Sometimes we look at children and we marvel at their ability to live in the present. We envy them. But we have a choice about that, too. We can actually stop and change our attitudes. When we see ourselves slipping into regret about the past or worry about the future, we can bring ourselves back into the present. Dwelling on the past or the future is of no value. It just tortures us.

When I go out to eat, I struggle with time. First of all, I have this thought that we have to get to the restaurant at a certain time. Of course, we don't; but even so, I get impatient. I keep thinking, "We're going to be late."

After we get in the car, I can't wait until we get to the restaurant. When we arrive, I can't wait until we get inside the door. We get inside the door, and the hostess says, "Just wait here; I will put your name down." Now I can't wait until our table is ready.

Finally, the table is ready. I sit down, and I can't wait until the server comes and takes our order. Then I can't wait until the food comes. When the food comes, I start eating the peas, and I can't wait until I get to the french fries. When I'm eating my main course, I'm thinking about dessert. And then I can't wait until we get the check, we can pay, and we can get back in the car to go home.

Have you ever done that? Have you ever spent an entire evening being just a little bit out of the present moment?

This example illustrates the whole experience of eating out, but missing every pleasure by just a few minutes. It's really hard to just eat the peas or drink the iced tea. It is hard to be in the moment instead of in constant anticipation.

EMOTIONS TIED TO THE PAST OR FUTURE

What are some negative emotions attached to living in the past or the future?

> Guilt
> Anxiety
> Regret
> Shame
> Sadness
> Fear
> Anger

I think we could find that every negative emotion is related to living in the past or in the future. And, of course, you can only live in the present. By trying to live in the future or the past, we still live in the present, but we spoil its quality.

A counselor was called to the bedside of a cancer patient because the nurses believed that the cancer patient couldn't handle the constant pain. The counselor sat with the patient and said, "What is it like?" The patient said, "Oh, it's awful. I have these terrible pains. I'm never free of pain, and I think I'm going out of my mind. I can't do anything. I can't think of anything. I'm always in pain."

The counselor said, "Are you in pain right now?"

The patient looked puzzled. She stopped and reflected, and then she said, "No, but I was a few minutes ago."

"What are you experiencing right now?"

"Well, nothing. But I'm going to feel some pain pretty soon."

The counselor continued to work with the patient, eventually making a map of the patient's pain. There was a burst of pain, then it subsided. Then a long time passed without pain. It turned out that the patient experienced two minutes of pain and then about twenty minutes without pain. Twenty out of twenty-two minutes, the patient was not in pain. Ninety percent of the time, she was pain-free.

She had believed herself to be in constant pain, but with the help of the counselor and by living in the present, she was able to get up out of bed and resume a normal life, pausing to deal with the pain as it came up.

Do you see what was happening? The pain was being magnified by remembering it and by anticipating it.

Jesus said, "Today's evil is enough for today." Pain is bad enough when you are experiencing it. Why worsen it by dwelling on it afterward or anticipating it ahead of time?

Looking to the future with anxiety and to the past with regret takes away all the happiness of life. So if you want to fully enjoy life, just learn to live in the present.

THE EIGHTH TASK

Whenever you feel regret or anxiety, observe any connection with the past or future, let go of it, and bring yourself into an awareness of something positive in the here and now. Say to yourself: "This present moment is eternity. I am in the perfect place at the perfect time."

REPORTING ON THE TASK

Leslie: This is a tough one, and I'm working with it a lot. I made a phone call to the person who's subletting my house back home, and right now she's doing renovations. She's not actually living there, and I'm stuck paying a phone bill. I finally threatened to turn the phone off, which got her to return my call. We had made an agreement, I thought, that she could repaint two or three rooms of the house, and I had said really emphatically that some other rooms I had just painted the way I like them, and if she was even thinking about changing that, would she please talk to me about it. She told me that she had repainted the whole house.

I remembered my task of being in the present moment, and I said, "Well, this is this moment. The house is already painted. I can't really ask her to clean the paint back off the walls. The paint's on the walls, and I'm in Tucson." And so I said to her, "Well, I'm trying to live in the present, so I guess the paint's on the walls, so I don't know what else to say about that."

I kept on being really distressed, and I finally worked out that I'm not at all distressed about what color paint is on the walls. I can't see them from here. I'm distressed about her not keeping her agreement with me. I'm realizing the reason I'm upset is because the agreement wasn't kept, and so now I'm projecting into the future all these other agreements that I think she's not going to keep, including paying the rent. Since it's a sublet, if she doesn't pay the rent, I'm responsible for the cost. So I'm already imagining hiring lawyers and trying to figure out how to deal with her, and it's all because of just a simple matter. She didn't keep our agreement.

So what I'm working on is figuring out whether and how to take that up with her. I don't want to do it in a way that makes enemies. I think my grief has been over feeling like I didn't do quite a good enough job of taking care of myself. And also over thinking that I left my house in the care of somebody I thought was a friend, and now that's challenged. So that was my moment of trying to be in the present.

I wish that right there, in the present moment, that I had been able to think through all of this, and be able to just calmly say, "We had an agreement. What happened to the agreement? Why didn't you check that out with me?" That would save me the pain of all this stuff that I've gone through since, thinking about how I'm going to talk to her about what happened.

Session Leader: Thank you. That is a very vivid illustration of how getting out of the moment is where the upset is.

Keri: Today I made a mistake at work, and filed something in the wrong file. One of the lawyers called me up—she's a young lawyer, not much older than me probably—and she said, "Can you come here and talk to me for a minute?" And right away I was pretty sure I'd done something wrong. I went in, and she said, "I'll shut the door," and I thought, "Great, shut the door." Then she said, "Well, I'm shutting the door because you made a mistake, and I didn't want to draw attention to it." I went back to my desk and started thinking, "All right, how many times can I do that before I get fired? Do other people do that?" Basically, I was imagining getting fired.

One morning I was driving to work, and I projected that when I got to work it was going to be really bad. Then I realized, "Okay, I'm not at work yet, so I can still enjoy the ride to work." I was just enjoying the ride and kept reminding myself, "I'm still driving to work." Then, as I walked into work, I was still imagining that it was going to be bad when I got there, and I kept saying, "I'm still walking to work, and it's nice." So I kept doing that, and it was a really long walk, you know? It isn't, really. It's only a quarter of a mile, but I was thinking, "Wow, think about how long I've been walking to work and haven't been at work." And it lasted just as long as I said it, and then everything would come back, but that crystal-clear split-second was beautiful.

Marie: I feel like I had such a full week. Looking at the progress I've made in my life, I just was astounded at how much I was able to be in the present moment, and still also see how far I have to go. On Monday, the father of one of my students committed suicide, so that brought up all this grief. The first day when I found out about it, it was just grief. Instead of being anxious about what I had to do that day, I just sat and made a card. It was a reminder to me to stay in the present moment and just be appreciative that I was still alive.

Then there was fear about, "What am I going to say to my student when he comes in?" I just would let that go and really be in the present moment about it. Just present with my feelings. And then when he did come in, I felt like I was able to be there. Not feel like, "Oh, I have to say this," or, "What shouldn't I say?" or, "What should I say?" Just be like, "Hi, how are you doing?" Breathing a lot was very helpful. I always notice when I'm getting anxious that I'm not breathing. Then as soon as I breathe, it's kind of like letting life in.

Janet: Living in the present has been difficult, for a while. I'm thinking about making a major change in my life, but not until after the first of the year. I see that if I do this, I have to do some legal work or something. And I find it really difficult to tell anybody that I'm close to about this, because it sounds so permanent. It's easier to tell just acquaintances what my plans are, or people I don't know well. I guess that gives me courage or something. But then I get real fearful. Anyway, I'm not in the here and now. If I do make this decision, I do have to do some legal and financial stuff. I get real stressed, and I breathe deeply to release the stress.

Frank: We were invited out to dinner at a really expensive restaurant. We got there and then we waited for our friends to arrive. And we waited and we waited. In the end, we waited an hour and three-quarters. So I had an hour and three-quarters to live in the present, which actually was really neat, because there was a lot going on. We kept just reminding ourselves it's very pleasant to sit in this beautiful restaurant and watch people go by. There was a wedding where people were dressed in medieval costumes, and so the groom was coming through in his doublets and hose. That was fun.

During that time, it was very nice to have a task that's about living in the present. The interesting thing is that later we found out that our friends were at a *different* restaurant, wondering about where *we* were. The restaurants had similar names. Anyway, the negativity really hit when we said, "We were really fools to sit at the wrong restaurant." It sort of took away the joy of being in the present. The reality is we had a great time sitting there. There was a musician, and we danced on the dance floor. And we went home and ate peanut butter and jam sandwiches.

The next day, we met the people and they took us out to a restaurant, and so we managed to catch up. We sat down to eat at 1:34, and the food got there at three. One of the slowest services I've ever had at a restaurant, but we got into such an interesting discussion it didn't matter that the food wasn't there. And every now and then I'd think, "Hmm, food hasn't come yet." But in the present, the conversation was just wonderful. The conversation was a feast, so who cared if the food got there? But I could imagine that it would have been very easy to slip into, "Where's the food?" and have the thing be about where's the food and why's the waitress so slow. But we had a great time. And there's part of me that wants to keep records and say: "Hmm, let's see: That was an hour and three-quarters on Saturday. Do I get a prize for being so patient?"

Stewart: It's funny that I find when it's the week to practice that task, I'll just rebel. I've been trying to practice living in the present moment for the last year or so, trying different techniques, and hearing different lectures on tape.

There were a few times when I used my lunch meal to do the task, which tends to be a rushing time because I trade off with my wife right at lunch and I go to work at one, and she comes home at a little after twelve, and I have to make lunch and then eat it and be gone at one. So I'm usually late. I usually find myself, at a quarter to one, sitting down and just wolfing my food. And I really tried to stay present this week, and just taste the food, the different textures of the food, and not think about the time.

It's interesting how my tendency, especially with children, is to notice that if there's a moment to eat, I try to get it all down on my plate because I know something's going to happen where I'm going to have to hop up anyway. So I've found that I just try to eat as quickly as possible, and then I say, "Wow, I don't even remember what the food was like in my mouth!" It just sort of went right down. It was interesting to try to maintain an awareness of the joys of the moment, and at the same time be a good parent.

Darren: The dishes were in front of me, and I was thinking, "Ugh, I don't feel like doing the dishes right now." And I suddenly realized, doing the dishes is impossible. I can do *a dish*, but I can't do *the dishes*. It's not something I can do all at once. So I just pick up a cup and put it back, or pick up a dish. It was strange; I got really into it, the idea of "I'm not even doing a dish, I'm doing this portion." The same thing with eating. I was beginning to think: "I'm eating pretzels. No, actually, I'm eating *a* pretzel. Not even a whole pretzel, but just part of a pretzel." And then the cool insight that came to me was, "Wow, these words almost take over the actions that I'm doing." To call it a pretzel, in a sense, is to get away from what it really is. It's like, "I'm eating wheat with peanut butter in the middle." I just got really into the whole thing. "I'm not chewing it; it's just in my mouth." It was pretty mental. It wasn't like experiencing it, but it was kind of getting close to it. Those were my best experiences in the present moment.

Elly: Yesterday I went to my boyfriend's church, and it's very spirit, revival stuff. It's very powerful, and I felt within myself, as soon as I walked in, just so much resistance, and almost disdain and negativity and judgment and condescension. Just terrible! I felt like a big black cloud coming in there. Then I just started to realize, "Well, I'm probably going to be sitting here for two hours, so I'm either going to be negative and be grumpy and think of a hundred different things I could be doing with my time right now, or I could just accept it and be part of it and be in the pres-ent, and not worry about what didn't get done." So I did that, and it was really nice, and I learned a lot from it.

There were benefits, and it was interesting because there was a part where some of the people in the congregation talk in tongues, so there'll be one person dancing across the room with a big wand and a big ribbon, and then there'll be little kids running everywhere, just having fun being little kids, which I really like watching. But then there'll be a few people just shaking, crying, and laughing. And I'm sitting there, and there's a couple of people that are looking at me, like, "Oh, she must be new. How are you doing?" So that was nice.

Then I was overcome with this feeling, like, "Oh my gosh, what if I marry this person, and what if I have to go to this kind of church for our whole marriage, and what if we have kids? Do I have to have my kids be a part of this?" I felt like I had been launched into the future, and was just being paranoid. I really felt myself freaking out about it. So he noticed that, and said something immediately about it, and I didn't even say anything. So we kind of talked about it a little bit. Then I was standing there, and I tried to sing along with one of the songs, because it was nothing out of the ordinary—it was just all about praise and worship, which is fine. But then someone came up from behind me, and they put their arms on my shoulders, and I couldn't see them, and they just whispered in my ear, "Well done, bless you." And my body stiffened up a little bit, because sometimes I can be weird about being touched. But then their hand kind of dropped to my back and touched my belt loop, which was weird because I was like, "Oh, you know, they're pulling me back in the present and I'm here in the room and I'm not freaking out." So I thought that was nice; it was a little reminder.

Noomay: The first night I had so much going through my mind, every feeling, every thought, everything I have to do. So I just decided to write it all out, and pages just went by. I was thinking I need a list for each category of things that I'm thinking about in the future, and things that I've been really feeling a lot of regret and shame and guilt for in the past. I was thinking I need to write more of them down. Then I went to sleep and woke up, and I noticed that I wasn't as worried in the morning. Which is something that I had noticed a lot for the past few weeks. It happens at certain points, I'll just wake up and a list of things will go through my mind. It was just nice to wake up and a negative thought would come to my mind, and I would hear it and then let it go. So that really helped that part of the day, throughout the week. It was a reminder to me.

The next day my fiancé and I were going to drop off the car, and they said it would take a certain amount of time, but it ended up taking a couple more hours. For part of the time we were waiting there, and we would leave and then come back, and they said, "Well, it's going to be at least another hour." At one point, we came back and they said, "Twenty minutes," and we thought, "Maybe we'll wait here." And I just was thinking, "Oh, I just don't want to be here. It's so terrible." Every seat was dirty, it was dark, and just terrible pictures on the walls, and I just felt like "ugh."

Then I remembered the task. I'm thinking, "This is exactly where I'm supposed to be, right here at this place that's come to me. This is perfect. A perfect place I'm supposed to be in." So I was like, "It's time to get a little more comfortable." I was listening to the two that were working there, thinking, "Wow, their accents are really enjoyable." I don't usually get to hear that Indian accent. It ended up being a really good day; we talked a lot about simple things. I can't believe how many things worked during the day from one moment to the next. That was fun just to appreciate and talk about it. Celebrate how beautiful it was outside.

Angus: I have a huge problem with it. It's just such an ingrained way of thinking for me. I *never* live in the present. It really made me think about it; like we were saying last week, sometimes you go to the future because there's something good to look forward to. The only reasons I ever go to the future are because I don't like the way things are right now, or there's something I'm totally afraid of in the future. I also thought that, this week, it would be a good task to do the opposite. Because I always go to the future and see something, and then spin a million negative outcomes on it. It would be good to live in the future but spin positive, like, imagine how many wonderful things could happen.

But by not living in the future, I eliminated *so* much negativity. I love this task! This is the most powerful thing, because it just prevented me from going down all these alleys. Well, I don't know what's going to happen. So I'd constantly be bringing myself back to the moment. I like that you had to find something positive, because that refocused my attention on something good. It was almost always something close, like "the sun is warm on my hand," or "it's nice there's a breeze." Just something like that. It was a good week to have this task. I had one of the most peaceful, positive experiences.

Greg: I found that I didn't spend time thinking about either future things that I need to do, or on past things that I or others have done. Focusing on being in the present gave a different context for those events. It's almost as if I'm in the present, thinking about something in the past, so I didn't compromise my "hereness." It's a nice way of getting a little distance from those things that lie ahead because, in a sense, I'm conscious of them in the present, but I sort of shift my focus so I'm trying to find ways of engaging those tasks in the future. I'm not just spinning and spinning and thinking about these eventualities that are out there. It's the same thing with the past. It was a nice way of holding them in the present, and so, therefore, getting a little bit of distance from my emotional involvement with them in the past. I wasn't in the past; I was sort of regarding the past from the present. It was an interesting shift of perspective. But in general, the challenge of trying to dwell in the here and now is one that I was pretty comfortable with.

Nicole: The first couple of days after we were assigned the task, I was definitely not at all in the present. I had just started seeing somebody a couple of days before the task and that really brought up a lot of stuff in the past about previous relationships and thinking about the future.

Bob: I have many things in my past that I wished wouldn't have happened, and I have many anxieties about the future. I don't know what I want to do with myself in the future, and that has a lot to do with why I have anxiety. The past holds many problems for me.

I've had business and legal problems. Family problems are the basis of much regret.

Since I don't know what I want to do with my future, I envision an existence of few challenges and fewer opportunities. I don't want to live in the past, but I do want to work on a better future for myself and my family.

When I worked the task this week, I found few moments of peace without the past or the future entering my thoughts.

Session Leader: When I find myself getting into one of those two states, I'll go through the five senses as a way of bringing myself into the present.

What am I feeling right now? I'm feeling the smoothness of the paper. I might just revel in that a little bit and explore the different textures.

What am I seeing right now? I look around. What am I hearing? What are the sounds? All of those have to be in the present, and it's a way of reversing the process of the negative thought that diverts you from the present.

I use the present to divert myself away from the negative thought. Even taste. What am I tasting right now? I find I can keep bringing myself back to the present.

There are some pitfalls with this technique, where you need to do work in the present to prepare for the future. It is called planning. Planning an event is totally different from doing the event.

It has its own joy, its own pleasure. It can be fun just to sit and plan.

Suppose you have two people, one of whom is worried about the future saying things like "I don't know whether to go to school or not. I'm totally stressed out!" The other person says, "Hey, this is fun. Let's get out some school catalogs. Let's look at the possibilities!"

One person is having fun and the other person is stewing. What is the difference between the two people? Why is one person enjoying it and the other person in a panic? One is living in the present and enjoying the process. With the other person, the element of fear is entering and disturbing the process.

TASK 9

Dealing with False Cause

Influx never takes place from the outside to the inside; it goes from the inside to the outside.
Emanuel Swedenborg, *Arcana Coelestia* 8322

It appears as if things in the world flow in through the senses towards the inner realms of the mind, but this is a false impression. The inner flows into the outer. Perception arises from that inflowing.
Emanuel Swedenborg, *Arcana Coelestia* 5119

WE OFTEN ASK our spiritual growth groups to list the things, situations, and people that upset them. One group wrote for about ten minutes about all kinds of things. Then they paired off and shared some of their answers with each other.

When they finished, I said to them, "I do not want to know what is on your lists, because the fact is that things, situations, and people do not upset us. They may provide opportunities for upset, but the cause of the upset is inside of us, not outside."

Their jaws dropped, and we got into a long and serious discussion, during which we reflected on the possibility that what they thought was upsetting to them was not the real cause of their upset. It could be called "false cause." This point is important because our spiritual development depends on our taking responsibility for our own reactions to outside influences.

The appearance that things outside us cause our reaction is very strong, and it is difficult to believe that external influences do not cause our feelings. When we are upset, we look for something in our environment, or to another person, as the reason for our upset.

This is not the real cause of our reaction, and so we call it false cause. Our states and moods actually come from inside us. If we are happy, it is because we choose to be happy. If we are upset, it is because we choose to be upset. Our mood is not the result of the situation, the people, or the things outside us.

Take an example: Suppose you are driving along in a car, feeling fine, when you stop at a red light. All of a sudden, you realize that the car behind you is not going to stop, and you're about to be rear-ended. Sure enough, you hear the crash. Now, you are mad. You're furious!

Why are you so furious? Because someone smashed into your car, of course! Your internal dialogue starts: "That blankety-blank person ought to be put in jail. Those lousy drivers make me sick!" You feel as though you're totally justified in being upset. Furthermore, you feel you *have* to be upset. You have no choice about it. It's because someone ran into you, right?

You get out of the car and are about to yell at the driver, when you realize he's slumped over the steering wheel. You realize that he is having a heart attack. What happens to your feelings? *Then* you discover that the man slumped over is your father! *Now* how do you feel?

The incident has not changed, but your feelings have because you see the situation differently. This means that your reactions are not caused by the accident, but by how you interpret the accident.

We make up things in order to allow ourselves to be angry. This is why we so easily jump to conclusions: "That person did that on purpose." "What a terrible driver." "He shouldn't be on the streets."

With all these reasons, we feel our anger is justified. We have a right to be angry. It is hard to realize that we are angry because part of us *wants* to be angry. Rage has found an opportunity to enter us. It has nothing whatever to do with what we think is the cause, such as the other person's driving. That just provides an opportunity for our anger to arise. It is not really the cause.

ANGER IS AN INSIDE JOB

Causes are not external; they are internal. Anger is always an inside job. Something outside might trigger it, but the feeling comes from inside.

I was in England when Queen Elizabeth II was being crowned. My cousin and I decided to sleep on the sidewalk that night, to make sure we'd have a good view of the coronation procession, which was at ten o'clock in the morning. At seven o'clock, a policeman woke us up. "All right, you blokes, on your feet!" Soon we were all standing, leaning forward, and straining to see what was going on. This was three hours before the coronation procession, but we were already shoving and pushing.

After some time, a woman off to my right said to the man behind her, "Would you stop shoving me!" The man said, "It's not me; it's those people behind me." She said, "But there is nobody behind you!" He turned around, looked behind himself, and saw that there wasn't. That is false cause.

Suppose that other people really *were* the cause of our states. This would mean that other people could make us happy or sad. They could put us in heaven or hell. All they would have to do is act badly, or yell at us, or talk too long, or not talk at all, or step on our feet, and they could put us in hell. No, the universe is not created that way. We put ourselves in hell.

If we are involved in spiritual work, we do not allow our emotions to be controlled by people, situations, and things outside of ourselves. We don't allow ourselves to be upset by what we read in a newspaper. What we read on a piece of paper can only upset us if we choose to be upset by it. Another person may look at the same newspaper, but not be upset in the same way. The upset is not the result of the newspaper. It is the result of something inside us. It is as if a little beast inside us says, "Now, it's time to be angry."

A man who was teaching fourth grade took this course and was fascinated with "false cause." He wondered if this would work with children.

One day a child came up to him and said, "Johnny made me so mad. He tore up my paper." The teacher corrected him and said, "Say, 'I made myself mad when Johnny tore up my paper.' Try that." The child looked puzzled for a moment, thought, and then said, "Yes, it's true. I did make myself mad when Johnny tore up my paper." He went back to his desk feeling much better.

How do you know that negative emotions are an inside job? A person can say something to you one day, and you're angry. He can say the same thing another day, and you laugh. He could say the same thing yet another day, and you have no reaction at all. You choose your own reactions. It is not the other person's fault.

What is upsetting you? Suppose you wake up, and it is raining. You might even tell someone that you are upset because it is raining. Yet some people love it when it rains. Is the rain the cause of one person's being upset and the other's being happy? The rain does not make you happy or sad. It is just rain. You can *choose* to be happy or sad when you see it rain. That is your choice. It is not because of the rain.

There is a wonderful story in the New Testament about workers hired at different times of the day. Some workers worked twelve hours. Some worked two hours. People hired at the eleventh hour only worked one hour, and then the working day was over. No agreement was made as to how much money these last workers would get.

The master paid these last workers first and gave them a denarius, which was the agreed wage for a full day's work for the first workers hired. The people who had worked all day began thinking: "They got a denarius. We must be getting much more." When the master paid them, they too received one denarius each. They were furious. Were they upset because they were paid the amount that was agreed? The master said: "Can't I do what I want? Is your eye evil because I'm good?" This meant: "Are you jealous because I'm good? I do you no wrong. I paid you what you agreed to receive" (Matthew 20:15).

The workers' upset was an inside job. They made themselves upset because they had fantasized about getting more.

It is amazing to think of life in terms of real cause versus false cause. I believe you can be in the most unpleasant surroundings and still be totally at peace, because your environment is not the cause of your reaction. You react the way you want to react. It must be added that we are not perfect, and there are some situations that trigger negative reactions. I know there are some situations in which I will probably feel upset. I will upset myself in these situations, but the situation is not the cause.

Your task this week is to observe your upset feelings from this point of view. Then notice how you feel.

THE NINTH TASK

Whenever you feel upset from a thing, situation, or person, stop and remember that upsets do not come from outside you, but from inside, and observe your reactions to the situation from that point of view.

REPORTING ON THE TASK

Keri: I had a doctor's appointment in the morning. I got done early so I was able to go out to breakfast with a couple of friends and still make it back to work by the time I had said I would be back. So my friend and I started to think about what we had to do next. I had to work and she had to go to painting class. We just weren't very excited by the prospect, and we had a really good time at breakfast. It was one of those things where you're having such a good time that it's harder to go to work than usual. But then we remembered the task, and I was like, "Okay, so there's nothing bad about work. It's all in my head." So when I realized that, it made me feel good because it made me feel like I have control over what happens to me today. Even though I don't have control over what I'm doing, I have control over how I look at it; and if it really doesn't matter where I am, then it can be really good. So I just felt better, and I didn't have any problems going to work.

Greg: I understand the task of being aware that one's reaction to events is not caused by the events, but by one's reaction to them. I guess I had imperfect success with that concept, because I still find myself clinging to the idea that, although my reaction to it may be my own, nonetheless, that reaction has been provoked. So basically, I may be angry about a state of affairs that someone else has caused, and of course, they aren't the ultimate author of that anger. I mean that anger is something that I may generate. But there are instances where it seems to me, still, that people have engaged in activities—whether they're directed against one personally or that are just sort of evil in the world—that excite those sorts of responses.

I found myself thinking, once I came to that conclusion, about that scene in the garden of Gethsemane, when the soldiers are coming to arrest Christ, and there's Peter with the sword, and he lops off the man's ear. That's I. And so I recognize that this anger is mine, and not excited by the event, because clearly that story shows that one can have access to a totally different response to aggravating circumstances. But I have not yet got myself to the point that I can set some provocations aside. I am going to wield that sword!

Janet: This one particular person at school is over-the-top about me; she has a really negative reaction. I always feel like I'm pulling knives out of my back when I leave there. And I finally realize that it's her issues that she's projecting onto me, and it's not me. But I still get upset, and I just go over and over. In fact, I'd planned to go up there after my first class this morning and confront her.

I was doing her a favor Thursday, because she wanted a copy of my notes. So she and another secretary were walking; she shanghaied me all the way on the other side of the campus. I happened to get up a little bit ahead, and when I looked back, she was making this little face with her jaw and her lips. I knew exactly that it was about me, and I was just stunned. She doesn't always wait until my back is turned to say something or do something. I don't think she saw that I caught that.

So she's just over-the-top, and I have to realize, "Don't get upset about it; it's her stuff." I got out of a lot of my upset by reminding myself it wasn't me. Kind of like what you said, Darren. How much of this upset is reality. What am I seeing? Is it coming from me?

Leslie: I worked the task about the sublease on my house again. I had just had to say, when this woman who moved into my house does this and that, it gets me upset. I just had to say, no, she didn't get me upset; I got upset. I would feel like there's a big hole in it somewhere. So what do I do with all these feelings that I have? They're still there. I still feel mad and scared and angry and desolate and upset, and all this kind of stuff. In nonviolent communication, we try to learn that every feeling that we have arises out of some need that we have. And it's not what the other person is doing, or what the situation is, that makes me sad or angry or feeling shame; it's because I have a need of some kind.

That sounds real simple, but what's the task to do about feelings? When something happens, I feel this way because I have a need for something. It could be something I wanted, or something that I value and cherish. It takes the focus off the other person, and puts it on what are the things I'm looking for in life. So if she lied to me about something that was taking place in my other house—which bit by bit I'm finding out from her more about some lies that she's told—I could make it all about her and how she should be a better person. And that's not too satisfying. Or I could try to turn it around and try to be just utterly compassionate and think, "Well, you know, I'm moving into a new house myself, I know it's hard, there's a lot of stress on you," and be forgiving. And that still leaves a big gap. If I can take that "I'm upset when I hear that, because I have a need of some kind," and work with it that way, that helps me.

I'm not so in-the-moment that I can do it right away. But if I think about it, or if I get with a group where we practice this task, I can get some help with it. I guess I have been angry, but trying not to let that drive how I deal with this person.

Noomay: In a big area of my life, I was very much reacting to another person. It brought up a lot of negativity in me. It took a day to really feel what I was reacting to. I realized, as I started reading the quotes on the task, what I needed to see—basically this person isn't making me upset. Then it came up, "Okay, these are needs that I'm having." At that point, I was putting the focus back on the needs that I was having, and the values and things that I believe in, and in self-worth things. So I was like, "Okay, I can't use my energy to react to this person negatively. I have to take care of these inside of myself, and I have these needs."

But I really felt helpless to them, so I was thinking, "I need to do something about this; I need to seek help." And right away, I was aware of something just in front of me, that I knew was a gift from the Lord. I was able to, throughout the week, let go along the way and be thankful that I have this place to get help. I ended up seeking the help, and it was just a big step. It was a great task to help push me a little bit further in that area, step outside of myself. Also, it triggered a bunch of reaching out to other people.

Frank: I got upset with somebody. I had to stop and say, "Now wait a minute, I'm upsetting myself."And then I noticed that I was making things up about this other person to be upset about. They probably weren't intending or doing anything harmful, but I sort of thought they probably were. "This person's probably doing this to hurt me." So I got upset not at the person, but what I was projecting onto the person; so it was nice to just say, "Oh, I'm upsetting myself. Hmmm." And the feeling of upset lingered; it wasn't as if it just totally went away, but at least it didn't allow me the luxury of going on and on and on about what this other person was doing, or intending to do.

Darren: The whole idea that nothing outside myself causes negativity really saved me this week. I went on a hike with a good friend. I was feeling sick, very irritable, and everything that came out of my mouth was negative. It was really promoting a very unhappy sphere, and yet I was convinced that the unhappy sphere was due to the other person's behavior, not my own. But I was only convinced on the outside, because I had the task. Internally, I knew that I was responsible for however I felt, and though externally that seemed impossible, I did my best to hold to that.

So the first action I took was to say to my friend that I wasn't going to say anything because I was powerless to my negativity, and that to speak would only fuel the fire of a fight. That caused a chance for reflection, rather than spewing out my inner reflections and trying to injure that person with them. I was able to observe more objectively.

The reason that saved the week for me was because a fight like that in the past could have led to a snowball effect that would lead to more and more fighting. Instead of creating two difficult hours, it would create three difficult *days*. Maybe even a really hard *week*. That's why I feel like it saved my week.

Marie: I remember there were three days where I was sure that I would be happy if only I could sleep in. I would wake up and just be like, "If only I could sleep in just a little longer; then it would be okay." But then, of course, I couldn't because my children woke up. Then I would spend the whole morning thinking, "If only I had been able to sleep in, I would be happy." Then I would say, "Oh, that's external cause. That's not true. You can be happy." And I'd know that for an instant, and then my pattern would go back: "I'm not happy because I didn't sleep in." It went on for three days, this struggle in my mind, and finally I realized that these thoughts were a lie. It finally got through to my core, and I was able to be happy without sleeping in.

Angus: Most of my situations where I get upset seem to happen at work. It's like I put myself in these situations. It's very unpredictable; I never know what's going to happen, because it's sort of a weird psychological game that goes on there. So something did happen, where I did something which seemed to me so logical, and it had to do with alphabetizing something. Then my boss said, "Oh don't be ridiculous; we don't have time to alphabetize things." I argued with him for about five minutes, "Of course we should do this!" He's really good at arguing. He sort of enjoys it, and is really good at maintaining his composure, while I, on the other hand, get all riled up and emotionally upset, and lose control over something really stupid.

Even after it's over for fifteen minutes, I'm still doing it. But then I was thinking, "Okay, he's not upsetting me; I'm upsetting me. And why am I upset?" When I got a little deeper into thinking about the situation, I realized it's because he's challenging what I feel is right. So it totally upset my equilibrium, my sense of being a good worker and good to have around. It's not so much the situation; it was just that he happened to attack a part of me that is not very secure.

Session Leader: We have to deal with many things in our life, and the appearance is very strong that these things cause us problems. Once I was talking with a group of people in this course. They were having a real problem with the whole idea of false cause, and one of them said, "Suppose someone was coming at you with a knife. Wouldn't that cause you to be upset?"

Before I had a chance to answer, someone else in the group said, "That very thing happened to me. I was leaving an apartment building and was suddenly faced with an intruder wielding a knife.

"The amazing thing is that as I looked at him and saw the flashing knife, it was as if time stood still, and I could hear myself thinking, 'Let's see. How should I react to this?' I knew that I had a choice, not just about what to do, but how to respond internally. I became very calm, and then moved aside very quickly as the knife fell.

"I think he was so startled by my calm reaction, that he took one last look at me and fled."

Obviously, it is very upsetting to have someone come at us with a knife. But even such a violent act is outside us. Even in such an extreme situation, we have a choice as to how to react.

TASK 10
Choosing Higher Delights

And Peter said, "Look, we left what was our own and followed you." And he said to them, "Truly I say to you that there is no one who has left house or wife or siblings or parents or children for the sake of the kingdom of God who will not receive many times more during this time, and eternal life in the age to come."

Luke 18:28–30

Stop from anger, and abandon rage; don't fret to the point of being in an evil state.

Psalm 37:8

WE EXPERIENCE PHYSICAL SENSATIONS, emotions, and deep feelings. We are multi-leveled beings, and this gives life richness and depth. Most of the time, these different levels coexist inside us without problems. They can support each other.

Imagine going out to a fine restaurant with a dear friend. Besides the pleasures of the environment and the taste of the food, there are the enjoyments of conversation and friendship. On even deeper levels, there may be feelings of well-being and peace.

There are other times in our life when these levels are in conflict with each other. Suppose we find ourselves at a wedding reception. The decor is beautiful, and fine music is playing. The refreshments are delicious, and people are having a good time. If, for some reason, we are depressed inside, we might feel empty and lonely even in the midst of a crowd of people. The inner feelings and the external situation do not match.

There are other times when we get caught up in some external pleasure at the expense of higher delights. We might find ourselves choosing a lower delight instead of a higher one.

Since each level of our life has its own pleasures or enjoyments, we have the opportunity to choose between lower and higher delights. One of the great problems with negativism, then, is that we get so much enjoyment out of a lower delight that it blocks us off from a higher one. The lower delight eclipses the higher one. There have been times in my life when I have wallowed in self-pity, feeling sorry for myself. I have allowed the negative enjoyment of self-pity to get in the way of making a move to be with other people and to enjoy their company. I preferred my own miserable company to the pleasure of being with others. I can also think of many times in my life when I made that little bit of extra effort and found that, in doing so, I experienced a much higher level of delight.

Late one Christmas afternoon, our family was gathered around the house. We had just finished a big meal and were all feeling lazy and lumpy, sitting there and wondering what to do. It would have been very easy to switch on the television, watch some mindless show, and fall asleep. But somebody in the family suggested that we should go out for a walk. The initial response was very negative. There was tremendous resistance.

After some discussion, we realized that you don't get much fun out of life unless you make an effort, and so we piled into the car and drove to a trailhead about six miles away. We were on the trail as shadows were lengthening toward evening.

The air was crisp and clear, and the golden setting sun was casting a wonderful light on saguaro cactuses decorated with newly fallen snow. Yes, it snowed that Christmas, which was very unusual for Tucson. We walked among the cactuses, watching the warm colors of the sunset reflecting off the snow. Our hearts were full of joy. We had a beautiful, refreshing walk, and when we got home, we congratulated ourselves on a wise decision.

We compared the invigorating experience of the beauty of nature to the numb pleasure that we would have enjoyed if we had stayed at home. We couldn't believe that we might have missed that opportunity. It's not that there would have been any serious crime in lazing around. It's just that we had chosen a higher delight, and we felt good about it.

Lower delights have their place in life. We need times of simple external pleasure. After a day's work, it is good to put up our feet, relax, and just enjoy the sensual part of life. If that was all we ever did, however, our lives would be lacking in the deeper pleasures.

Once I was sitting in a restaurant. I looked over and saw a person near me eating an enormous meal. The food was piled high on his plate. After the main course, he ordered a horrendous dessert, and I thought to myself, "This man is choosing the pleasure of taste over the delight of having a healthy body. The external, physical delight of eating is getting in the way of the superior delight of having general good health."

Then I noticed that I was choosing the lower delight of criticizing my neighbor, passing judgment on someone I didn't even know, over the higher delight of loving and honoring him. The part of me that enjoys being contemptible of others and feeling superior was overeating its own particular delight. It was a very low level of pleasure.

Once, when I told this story, a friend of mine said, "You know, I was in a situation just like that, only I sat and talked to the guy. After getting to know him, I really came to love and honor him, and I thought if this is the worst he does, he's doing okay, considering the various things he might have to deal with in his life. It was nothing compared to some of the other things that came out when he told his life story. I got to experience love for this person."

Some people get caught up in promiscuity. They enjoy having many different sexual partners. But compare the delight of making love to a series of strangers to making love as part of an ongoing commitment to someone you love. One of the problems of promiscuity is that external delight robs people of higher delights.

There is something very addictive about lower delights. Take, for example, teenagers who get caught up in shoplifting. They may feel a rush of excitement and glee from getting away with something illegal. Plus, they enjoy having things that they might not otherwise be able to afford.

Sometimes people who do "bad" things do so simply because they enjoy them. So what is wrong with that? There are two obvious answers:

1. By engaging in their behavior, they are hurting other people.
2. By indulging in the lower delights, they are missing delights of a higher order. In the case of shoplifting, for example, they are blocking the satisfaction that comes with making an honest living.

MORAL STANDARDS

People who have moral standards and try to live honestly have a satisfaction in their lifestyle that is on a higher level than the joy others experience in deceit and fraud. They are more at peace with themselves, and they experience higher levels of delight.

Why do some people fight with others? No doubt there are many reasons, but a very simple one may be that it is fun to get mad. If the other person has done something outrageous, that makes the fighting seem to be justified. It's even more fun. Yet it robs them of the deeper satisfactions that come with living peaceful and sensitive lives.

We all know people who are chronic fighters. It seems that they always find reasons to be in a fight. If things get too calm, they must stir them up. Why do they do this? They might simply enjoy it. They might even say, "What's wrong with it?" And the simple answer is that, by indulging in their love of upset, they are robbing themselves of higher pleasures.

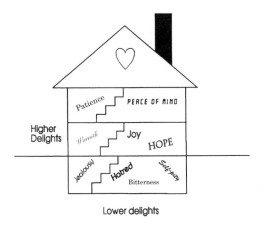

Higher
Delights

Patience   PEACE OF MIND

Warmth   Joy
            HOPE

Jealousy   Hatred   Self-pity
            Bitterness

Lower delights

THE TENTH TASK

When you suspect that a state you are in is negative, notice whatever enjoyment you may be having from it. What is the payoff for the negative state? What higher enjoyment is blocked by the negative delight? Let go of the negative and see if you can allow the positive to take its place.

REPORTING ON THE TASK

Nicole: I remember once I was feeling a lot of self-pity. I was trying to figure out why it was enjoyable. I had a hard time trying to figure that out. I guess the enjoyment I could really see was maybe just to get pity from other people by talking about it. I thought that by holding on to that, I was blocking the peace of the present moment. Just trying to think about it, I figured out to let go.

Stewart: My big day was on Sunday. We had tickets to see a musical, and I'd asked one of my friends to baby-sit. Right at the last

minute, she called and said, "Well, I'll baby-sit, but I'm not going to be there for part of it. I'll maybe have to be late and leave
early." This was through my wife that I heard this. It was sort of
a pattern. I felt so trapped into all these different emotions: resentment, premeditating. I talked about it with my wife, and we
said, "We're lucky just to go, and we'll work it out."

We were going to meet at the park to drop my kids off, and it
kept getting worse and worse. The friends that were going to baby-
sit were late; and when they showed up, they had their dog but
no car. They had walked there. One of our friends asked, "So you
didn't bring the stroller?" We were already late to the play, and
it became this super-complicated thing. She'd left a message on
the machine: "Bring a stroller, and I'm going to walk back to the
apartment." We had to do this car swap and drive around.

I was just starting to delight in it. "So! I have all the right in
the world to be so angry and resentful to this person." And then
I thought, "Well, actually I don't." I kept waffling back and forth,
and thought, "Oh, this is great! Everything's lining up perfectly
so that I can enjoy feeling so self-pitying. I don't even get to go
to a play." Then I just kept talking about it and thought, "This is
a great time to do the task, and if we miss the beginning, we can
listen to the CD at home." It turned out, after all that, driving to
find parking, and walking a mile, we missed only about three
minutes of the performance. And actually, I hate waiting in the
theater before the performance; I hate arriving early and having
to wait, so this was great. Someone actually volunteered to take
up the slack at the end of the performance and baby-sit.

Greg: My experiences weren't dramatic, but it was sort of a con-
tinuous realization that I tend to indulge in the pleasures of self-
righteousness when others are driving badly, or whatever it might
be. All those small irritations that allow me to point my fingers
at others and treat them with the scorn that they deserve. What
I came to realize is that it's basically pretty stupid, and I
found it was so easy just to let it go, because the task had com-
pelled me to be conscious of those moments of enjoying the finger-
pointing and the jeering. And just to set it aside was such a

pleasure, because it really is quite literally true that when your mind is occupied with that, it can't be occupied with something that's probably very pleasant that's there to be enjoyed.

Klara: I had a little difficulty with identifying what it was that I enjoyed, because when I'm thinking negative thoughts, it doesn't feel like I'm enjoying it because usually I'm feeling angry, and I don't really enjoy that feeling. The best thing I could come up with is that a lot of my anger is based in self-righteousness. "I don't like what this person is doing, and I'm so much better than this person because I would never do that." Or, like when one particular family member tends to hang onto things in the past, and I've always prided myself on not doing that, so I listen to their ways and think, "Well, if you just let go of the past, you know." So I guess it's the self-righteousness that I enjoy. My response was usually anger, and I don't enjoy that, but I guess what I get out of that is feeling like I'm totally justified in my anger.

Session Leader: How about the question of what it's blocking? Were you aware of what that anger blocks?

Klara: I don't know if I can really articulate it. I have a feeling that it's like, "I want to hang on to this self-righteousness. I don't want to let go of it."

Session Leader: And what's the self-righteousness blocking? May I make a suggestion? The joy of loving people is often blocked by the joy of judging people.

Klara: I guess that's what I mean when I say I'd have to admit that they're okay. I would have to love every aspect.

Session Leader: Sounds a little grudging. Is it?

Klara: Yeah, yeah. Definitely a little grudging. I'm going to be working on that.

Session Leader: I'm just suggesting you might actually enjoy it.

Frank: I had quite a week. We flew back to church headquarters to perform a wedding, so that was very useful, very pleasant. Flying back on the plane, I had a window seat and my wife was sitting behind on the other side on the aisle. There was a teenage boy to my left and his grandma, and we got to talking on the plane. I learned that this is only the second airplane flight he'd ever taken in his life, and the previous one was just an hour before that! So he was all eyes. He'd never been out of New York state, and now he was going to the big Wild West, and I had the window seat. And finally it dawned on me, "Think of the difference between his enjoyment looking out that window, and mine." So we traded places. And it was fun to see his reaction as the West unfolded below him, and seeing the irrigation circles and things he'd never seen before. So it really enhanced my enjoyment of the trip—I wasn't really giving up anything at all.

Marie: As soon as I heard that phrase *enjoying your negative emotions*, I was very aware of all the delight in these negative emotions. I have a plethora of things I could talk about. This week my hours were reduced at work, so basically someone's replacing me and taking over four of my kids at work. Immediately I felt like painting this picture of non-reality of this person who's replacing me being this evil woman that has used her power to replace me, and how nobody appreciates me, and all this stuff that I know is not true. Then I would let go of that and say, "You know, it's okay that I'm working less hours. I have more time to spend with my children and my family. I've felt overwhelmed, like I can't clean my house. It's nice that this is happening; this is a blessing."

But then immediately I would also go into a flip-flop. There's so much delight in being in the negative and painting this picture, like "Poor me! I'm the center of the universe. Everybody should feel sorry for me. All this struggle I have to go through!" And then realizing that none of that's true, I have a wonderful life, and it's all a blessing, and being grateful. So I definitely see that, when I'm in the negative, it's blocking all this wonderful happiness.

I love the phrase *God, free me from the bondage of self*. I just said that probably a hundred times a day, every time I'd get into this "poor me." As soon as I let go of "poor me," I'm free to enjoy the world, where I am free.

Keri: I want to read something that I wrote when I was waiting in line and I was going through a really hard time. I just read it again today, and it struck me as so funny. I just want to share it, because it's when I'm in that self-pity: "I am my own unfortunate circumstance lending tragedy and misery to any incomprehensible reality that I perceive." I think I wrote it in earnest. I really felt that way! [laughs]

Then there was a night when I went to happy hour with some people, and I thought about the task because usually I drink one beer, and they say, "Have another beer," and I say no, and they order me another beer. And I usually drink it. I didn't want that to happen. But I did have one beer, and that's pretty much enough to seal the fate for the evening. I went home and I was tired, and I thought, "Oh, I'll watch TV, because I'm so tired and there's nothing else I can do." I chose Garth Brooks over a sitcom, which I figured was like a little higher. [laughs] I only caught fifteen minutes of it, so then it was like, "Okay, should I watch this really stupid show that I don't want to watch at all, or should I just see if something else can rejuvenate me or somehow miraculously make me come alive again."

I just sat at my table, and I lit a candle, and I just observed. I wrote observations of everything that was going on around me, just of the nice picture—the candle was lit, Peter Gabriel's playing. Had this nice peaceful moment. I actually started reflecting, finding that I was alive, and I still had power in me and actually felt pretty good. Then I had a nice phone conversation with somebody, and I didn't think that I would be capable of that, but I was. So that was good.

I had a couple of observations. One was that I'm afraid that, if I turn away a lower love, there won't be a higher love to fill it up.

So that's something that I think about, and I guess I decide sometimes, "Oh, nothing's going to come. God isn't there, so I will choose a lower thing." I wrote, "The emptiness of the moment can feel like too much to have, but it's only fear coming in to take away what is precious in life."

Angus: I had a situation at work where I was being critical at someone. The other person I work with is consistently late, every day. Four minutes late, or five minutes, while I am always on time. I try to be on time. I pride myself on that. So for a while, I didn't notice that she was coming in late. But then the other day she came in late, like ten minutes late. My boss and I were standing there. I just wanted to say, "Well, I guess she's just not here yet, huh?" Just to make sure that he would notice, too. So I was trying to zip it up, and I just couldn't do it. I just went, "Well, she's not here yet." Then it was funny; he couldn't think of anything to say about that, so he said, "Yeah, is she gaining weight?"

Then I just realized, "Okay, this is not about her being late; this is just about talking negative things so you feel like a cool little clique because you're not like them." It was funny, like you have to say something negative, even if it's not relevant to the material. I just thought that's so funny that he said that.

But the payoff is that it makes me feel that, if I can judge other people, then it brings out qualities about myself that I feel are good, the opposite of their bad qualities. But the higher enjoyment was really obvious. It was just that I couldn't enjoy just loving another person, and being open to the moment. I was stopping that by making her "the late employee."

Darren: I've been physically sick, and that really took up a lot of my attention. But I did have some delight in the fact that I was sick. Like I would say to my brother-in-law, "Oh man, I'm worried about tonight, doing this demo, because I'm sick." I called up friends to go to the lecture, saying, "I'm not feeling too good, I need support." And I felt sort of delighted that I was sick, because if anything went wrong, I'd have an excuse. I could say, "Well, I was sick." And that blocks honesty, in a sense. What I really was saying was, "I'm worried, because I'm insecure. I'm worried, because I don't have enough self-confidence." Instead, I said, "I'm worried because I'm sick."

Another time during the week, I was talking to a good friend of mine. Their father and mother had been divorced, and I was saying how great I thought their father was. That felt very delightful, just praising that person. So I was in touch with a nice high delight, but that quickly changed when I said, "How could someone want to divorce him? How could someone not want to be with him? He's just the greatest guy." And I was about to make the case how unfair it is that he was divorced, because he was dedicated to the marriage, and it was wrong, and he should still be married. I was going to turn him into the victim, and turn his partner into the victimizer, which, of course, is very unfair and comes from a biased opinion. So the success for that was, I never verbalized any of that.

Session Leader: When people are treated poorly, they have been wounded. Then other negative feelings gang up on them and make the situation worse.

But that's exactly what happens in the body when you cut yourself. There are all these little germs that say, "Good, now is a chance to attack!" And in they come. They don't care about you; they just want to live. They like to live in wounds. Negative things cluster around wounds.

Remember, the beasts are in the basement. There's something about living in the basement where it's dark and miserable, but at least you *know* it. And you feel like you're supposed to be there. And then when you get up into a high room and the sun's coming through the window, you feel uncomfortable. "I've gone for a whole day without complaining, what's wrong? Nothing's gone bad today, what's wrong?" It's almost as if you need to get back in the basement to feel comfortable because there's that part of you that says, "I belong in the basement. I'm being punished for something." But, remember, it's not *you* that likes the basement.

What is the part of you that likes the basement? It's certainly *not* the part that likes the attic. That part is full of peace and love. It's a different part. So instead of making that part wrong and saying, "You're wrong to like the basement," you don't identify with that part of you. That is not the real you. It's just something that people have, like acne. You still *have* it, but it's not you.

Then you don't have to have a sense of breaking a rule by being happy. You're just going to experience that part of you that already *is* happy.

TASK 11
Forgiving Others

Forgive us what we owe, just as we've forgiven those who owe us.

Matthew 6:12

The kingdom of the heavens is comparable to a king who wanted to settle accounts with his servants. And as he began to settle, someone owing ten thousand talents was brought to him. But he was not able to pay it off, so the master commanded that he and his wife and children and everything he had be sold to pay it off. Therefore the servant fell down and worshiped him and said, "Be patient with me, and I will pay it all back to you." And the master of that servant had compassion and released him, and forgave him the loan.

Matthew 18:23–27

But if you don't forgive people, your Father won't forgive your blunders.

Matthew 6:15

Why wouldn't the Lord do the same?

Emanuel Swedenborg, *True Christian Religion* 539

WHEN SOMEONE HURTS US in some way, a message flashes inside our brain: "You will pay for this." Together with this, we have feelings of resentment and anger. We pull back and wait for some sign of repentance before we trust that person again.

In this experience, you will notice that there are two sources of pain. The first is the blow itself. It could be a physical injury, an insult, a theft, or something wrong done to someone we love. The second is the burden of inner feelings of resentment, bitterness, and revenge.

Sometimes we even say things like "I want you to suffer as much as you have made me suffer." Usually we really mean, "I want you to suffer *more* than I did."

I can remember my reaction to bullies when I was a kid. Once, an older boy shoved me into the gutter. In my mind, I began picturing the bully being subjected to all kinds of torture and pain. I wanted him to get worse than I got. What would it take for us to let go of those inner feelings? Would we be satisfied if the person apologized? What would it take for us to erase the message "You'll pay for this"? Would we forgive the other people if we saw them in pain? Would they have to weep and grovel on the earth before we let go of our anger?

Forgiveness sometimes relates to very small incidents. I can remember being in a meeting where someone made an insulting remark about what I was doing. I was furious. In my heart I said, "I can't forgive that."

The remark was said in only twenty seconds, but I carried resentment about it for twenty years! The strange thing is that I somehow thought I was punishing the other person for his remark. Who was I really punishing?

Suppose, at the time, I had said to a friend, "I am going to let that go. I forgive him." The friend might have turned around and said, "You can't let him get away with that kind of remark!" That is deadly advice. It encourages us to hold on to resentments for years.

Resentment is like a ten-ton weight on our head. Forgiveness is a way of letting go of that burden of resentment. When we forgive we, in effect, say, "You don't owe me anything. The debt is paid in full." This is hard to do without prayer. One prayer that I find helpful is: "Lord, forgive me for the many unkind things I have said to other people. Relieve me from bitterness about what other people have said to me."

In Matthew 8: 21–35, Jesus tells a parable about forgiveness in which a servant owed a king ten thousand talents. A talent was a hundred pounds of silver. In today's money, ten thousand talents would amount to tens of millions of dollars. The servant pleaded with the king for patience. He promised to pay the entire debt (although how he could possibly do it is another question). Eventually, the king "forgave" the debt—he considered it paid in full.

But then this servant went out and refused to be merciful to a fellow servant who owed him one hundred denarii. A denarius was a day's wage, so that was not a small sum. In our money, a hundred denarii would be the money earned in about four months of work. But compared to ten thousand talents, it was nothing.

In the parable, the servant refused to be merciful to the fellow servant who owed him one hundred denarii and threw him into prison. When the king heard, he was furious and reimposed the debt of ten thousand talents.

The amount owed to the servant by his fellow servant represents the injuries done to us by other people. They can be light or very serious. The ten thousand talents owed to the king refers to the indebtedness we have to our Creator.

In the case of my story, the one hundred denarii debt was the unkind remark someone else made about what I was doing. What was the larger debt? The ten-thousand talent debt was my twenty years of resentment, a ten-ton weight. How many ten-ton weights do people carry around with them unnecessarily? By forgiving others, we also unburden ourselves.

FORGIVENESS DOES NOT MEAN APPROVAL

A few years ago, I heard an interview on the radio. The woman being interviewed had been raped, and the rapist also blinded her so she could not testify against him.

I was amazed by her positive attitude. So was the interviewer. Finally, he said, "This man did two terrible things to you, and yet you seem to be completely free of resentment." The woman replied, "He had a half an hour of my life, and that is all he gets."

Evidently she had made a specific effort to let go of dwelling on him and his crime. In forgiving him, she was freeing her life up to be about other things.

Forgiveness does not mean approval. It does not say, "What you did was all right." It simply says, "I am not going to stand in judgment over you or wait for you to repay me for what you did."

Does this mean that people should be allowed to get away with murder? No, there is value in having a criminal system with appropriate punishments. It means that we need to be willing to leave judgment to God. This is because we know our own faults and shortcomings. Instead of putting energy into keeping accounts about other people's wrongs, we will put it into asking for God's forgiveness for our many shortcomings and errors.

The Lord's prayer includes the phrase *forgive us our debts as we forgive our debtors*. This implies that if we are not willing to forgive others, we are not in a position to ask for forgiveness. When we have been injured, instead of getting caught up in judgments and condemnation, we can use that as an opportunity to ask forgiveness for our own trespasses.

THE ELEVENTH TASK

When a person trespasses against you, use effort and attention to recall something you would ask the Lord to forgive you for. Hold them side by side.

REPORTING ON THE TASK

Elly: I wrote about forgiveness. It was just a very difficult one for me, and I'd like to pass on this report.

Darren: As for the trespassing, it was a good one for me because I'm in a twelve-step program and I'm on the ninth step, which is apologizing. So I'm very in touch with wrongdoings I've done and ways in which I've trespassed other people. Mapped it out very clearly. That's been a very useful tool.

I was really able to let go totally of resentments I had held towards one person, but some other subtle ones would come up. I'd think, "You know, this person has this problem and that problem," and immediately my defects would come up and show themselves side by side, and I'd go, "Oh wow, I am totally there; I've done the same thing," and could see that, unless I forgive that person, I'm really not also forgiven myself. Or allowing myself to be forgiven for the things I've done. And to release resentment is just so wonderful. I feel so much lighter, and just truly happy.

Another thing happened: I was in a social gathering, and there was a woman who was incredibly angry with her child. As she walked by, I actually went, "Oh my gosh," and she turned and looked at me and saw that I said that. Because I was sort of alarmed. It was a really cool process, because at first I was totally ready to be self-righteous and think, "That person is terrible." And I could see that, when I first got my dog, it was doing all sorts of things to the yard. I literally got that upset. I was like, "Ugh! Why did I get this dog? I wish I didn't have it!" And rage would come up. I could go, "Oh, I'm just like this person." And they were very clearly manifesting upset, and I suddenly thought that person was probably saying, "*Help*. I need help. Somebody offer me some help because I'm powerless." I'm just making this up, of course, but I sort of felt that maybe they were pleading: "I need someone to help me out with my kids right now. I need a break, but I don't know how to ask." So to go from being self-righteous and thinking a person's bad to shifting and seeing my trespasses and offering love was a really beautiful transition. God really gave me the gift of being able to feel it.

Session Leader: Could I just comment on "you made it up," because all of our reactions, we're making up stuff about the other person, whether it's negative or positive. We might think that the negative reaction is based on the truth and the other is based on the fiction, but it's really all fiction, isn't it? Do we really know another human being and can we really judge them? And so it's kind of neat if you make up something that leads to a positive result, compared to making up something that leads to a negative result.

Keri: A friend of mine that I spend a lot of time with had another friend in town, so I didn't get to see as much of them as I like. I felt hurt. I was going to go into that mode of "I'm hurt," and hold on to it. For some reason, it was valuable to me. I just remember being in my car, and I was thinking about it and thinking about the task. I also was planning on being super-independent and not needing anybody. I was going to go dancing, and maybe have a couple of drinks. I was going into that whole mode where I was totally separating myself from people, and something about that felt good. Then I realized, "Wouldn't it be so much nicer for everybody if I just concentrated on loving this person instead of being hurt?" I could feel a shift, a little shift, because I got excited about that idea. It seemed more legitimate than being hurt. I was like, "Okay, cool."

It was very interesting to watch myself. I would go back and forth between the two realities, and they were both really strong. The one that was pulling me back was pretty strong. It's like I had a lot invested in that reality or something. I went a little overboard because I was trying so hard to be loving and good that I really didn't give voice to my hurt feelings. So it was interesting to try to find a balance. I realized I really do need to say, "You know, I really do have hurt feelings, and I'm feeling really sad, and I need this." And it felt really good to be honest and feel those feelings, and realize I could feel that, and I didn't have to be super-independent. I mean, amazing things happened because of that. Whereas I might have sort of isolated myself, I ended up actually getting together with my friend and her friend, and really liking her friend and having a great time with them both. It was miraculous, I'd say.

Angus: Almost every week I talk about doing spiritual work and it happens in my car, on the road. Every time I would find myself wanting to get angry at somebody for cutting me off. Sometimes people are not even doing anything to me; they'll just be driving in a way that I don't think they should be driving. They could be down the road cutting somebody else off, and I'll go, "I can't believe they're doing that." I get really angry about it. And then I really did realize that I was that person a lot during the week. I'd be trying to get through a yellow light and somebody would come at me and I'd scoot in front of them and I'll go, "Phew, I hope they forgive me, because I'm that guy who's driving like a bad person."

On a higher level, I have some grudges that I've been holding. It's really difficult. I find that I can do spiritual work in my head, and it helps for me to try to understand their position and to always understand that nobody wants to be bad or do bad things. But it's really difficult to actually forgive from the heart. I find that I can do it and say it, but then a few days later I'll feel that old grudge. So I think it takes persistence. With big stuff, maybe you don't get it right away. You don't just forgive them the first time. It's like quitting smoking: you've got to keep trying to do it.

Klara: One of my early insights in the week was that I find it a lot easier to forgive somebody that I'm in touch with, like a family member, sisters, or someone I'm in an intimate relationship with. I have a lot of experience over the years with that, even if it's something fairly heinous. There are sort of little grievances that come and go, and I find those pretty easy to let go of. If it's something worse where I really was hurt, it takes a little longer. But I don't find it particularly challenging I guess because I know that I love that person, and that helps me get through it. It passes, it dissipates, I don't really have to focus on it, because I usually can see that they didn't really mean any harm and that they may, in fact, be sorry.

But I realized that people that I don't love, never did love, had no intention of loving—that is really, really hard. It's like forgiving somebody in this big void. You're never going to get acknowledgment from them that they hurt you, never any kind of apology, just this thing that happened that you still are feeling bad about, and it just seems impossible.

I look back at my past, and think of who are the criminals that I've had to forgive. I guess I don't have any real . . . well, maybe one or two conscious acts of forgiveness, but mostly I feel like it's something that dissipates over time. I had sort of let myself off the hook and said, "Well, I keep dwelling on this; I'm not going anywhere. I'll just tell myself it'll dissipate over time."

So I'm disappointed that I still haven't gotten very far. I guess I did—it gave me a chance to reflect and see that I've made some progress in certain aspects. I'd forgiven lesser parts of the whole, and that was encouraging. And also it was encouraging to realize that I'm not a totally unforgiving person, that I have a pretty regular practice of forgiving people that are in my daily life that I really care about. But it's a real challenge for me if I don't particularly care about this person, and I can get away with not really having a relationship. It's not somebody I'm forced to have a relationship with, yet I hold on to this. And, of course, it brought up a lot of stuff about what I've been taught about forgiveness: holding onto grudges, or just kind of being vengeful.

I realized I haven't probably had the best examples in my life. In fact, I can remember even as a little kid thinking, "Man, I hope I don't ever have somebody I don't forgive for thirty years," because that seemed like such a long time. But I was thinking about this particular person, "I could see that going for like a decade." It's a real reality check. So I'm going to keep working on this task.

Session Leader: I want to comment on the link that you're making between if you like the person, then you can forgive them. And I'm thinking, is there any real connection between forgiveness and whether you like or you don't like the person? Isn't it just as easy to forgive someone you don't like as someone you do like? There may not be any significant link there. The task about forgiveness is learning to let go of a resentment whether you like the other person or not.

Leslie: I'm just thinking about that, and I can see how it is the way Klara said, and then again, I think maybe it works a different way in my own life. It's with people that I care the most about that I have a really hard time letting go of resentments. If the person doesn't matter that much to me, then it's not a big deal; but if it's somebody that I really care about, then I want them to just shape up and act exactly the right way.

I was glad that the task said to me, when there's somebody in my life who I'm having a difficult time forgiving, to focus my attention on something I've done that I'd like to be forgiven for. Because that way I didn't have to come to terms with, "Do I forgive this person at this point or not?" But more just turn my attention to, "What do I wish I might be forgiven for?" That was really painful. I don't enjoy looking at them or thinking about them. It's difficult for me to look at those things, so it's kind of like cold water in the face. And maybe I didn't even get too deeply thinking about it, but it would certainly take my attention away from that other person that was so unforgivable. Like cold water in the face to stop and think, "Oh yeah, I've got a few of my own." So that's how I worked this week.

Marie: Tonight, the Lord gave me an opportunity to really work on the task. I was going to get the TV for my daughters, because they get to watch TV when they're being baby-sat. And all of a sudden I hear my older say, "I'm not going to tell you what I did! I'm not going to tell you what I did!" And I'm thinking, "Oh no! What happened?" I come into the room where they are, and my other daughter is on the floor, just doing this silent scream. I pick her up and I'm holding her, and she begins screaming for real. My older daughter's just crying and screaming too, just this mantra of "I'm not going to tell you what I did!" So I'm thinking, "Now what could she have done?" And I guess all the fear in me, I really wanted to switch the fear into blame and be like, "What did you do? How could you do that?" And really attack on my older daughter.

But I was able to separate myself enough from that and just calmly ask, "You know I love you; could you tell me what happened? Did she hit her head?" And she just kept going on this mantra, and it became clear that she had pushed her off the couch, and my younger daughter had hit her head. But then we just did all the things—like I remember my father talking about the difference between zeal and anger, and zeal is protecting the thing that's hurt, and anger is lashing out at the thing that did the hurting. I was able to, with help from this task, think, "Oh, now is an opportunity to forgive and just really be there for both daughters," because my older was obviously so sorry for what she had done. And she didn't need me to make her feel more guilty. So having thought that, we were able to talk about it, and I said, "So did you push her off the couch?" And she said, "How did you guess?" It's like, "Well, mommies know everything." But later in the car she confessed. It was obviously just weighing down on her. I said, "Well, thank you; that's very brave to tell me." I told her two stories about when I had hurt people. I'm very thankful for this task, because I feel like it saved my daughter from some blame.

Stewart: Like Klara, on my mom's side, I have this gene. I come from a long line of people who are like characters in an Ingmar Bergman film. They can hold a grudge for thirty years and die never speaking to their son again, for some slight infraction at a Christmas dinner party or something. But I get to see it played out in my extended family a lot, so I've been trying to work on it over the last few years. And I feel as though I have three levels of grudge. There's this sort of daily grudge I can give up right away, like I didn't get enough sleep last night and went to bed at midnight, and then my daughter at 5:30 in the morning says, "Dad, I'm hungry." I have so much resentment and hold a grudge all day. "I wouldn't be tired if I'd been able to sleep longer." But I can give that up fairly easily.

Then I feel as if there's a second level, like when my father and I got in a big argument. We talked about actually pairing off, getting in a fight. He apologized that afternoon, and it took me seven years to forgive him and to let go of that grudge. I felt really free of that during this week. I don't have a lot of that baggage.

Greg: I found the most helpful lever on this was thinking about those things done and undone for which I felt the need for forgiveness. I found myself, once I had that idea in my head, the next step was to say, "But I know that I am sincerely contrite for the things that I have done," in the sense that I have examined them, been conscious of the way in which they hurt others, and have done all that I can to make sincere acts of contrition and to start moving in different ways.

But then the next stage of the thought process was, "Well, how can I ever know how my own acts of contrition are received?" It's sort of presumptuous in a way to suppose that I can know enough about my own acts of contrition, or indeed how they are regarded, so that I can say, "Aha, I am differently situated from this person who may never have acknowledged their wrongdoing, because I know that I've done right."

In a sense, any hope that you have for being forgiven depends upon something that you can never know the answer to, and that is the adequacy of one's own efforts at contrition and atonement. You really have no choice, if you want to have any hope for forgiveness yourself, other than to extend that benefit of the doubt and to realize that you are in all respects identically situated to that person who you may have been incapable of forgiving, or so my thoughts were running.

I began with that in hand; it was a useful tool for thinking about some particular issues. I had a person who was a very dear friend of mine years ago, and I had been harboring bad feelings that I think, if anything is justified, these were. But I began to think about it in light of my thought processes that I've just described, holding up that episode and my own feelings about them, just to see how I felt over the course of time. I'd engage it, re-engage it, re-engage it, just to see, as I conjured this person up in my imagination, what associations attached themselves to it. And I found that the rancor that had been there for so long just didn't seem to have a place for itself anymore. And it wasn't as if I got completely there, but some of the heat, some of the sense of self-righteousness, had in fact not been able to survive this earlier process of thinking. I think, though, it will be an ongoing process.

It may be a useful discipline to conjure up those events from time to time, and just see how they look. I can't help but have the feeling that, as time unfolds, it really will get to a point where something like full cancellation happens. You just realize that there's nothing there at all.

Frank: One of the things I've noticed is that, having done this task many times, there are so few resentments hanging around in my life. It's really nice. I was looking for them and didn't see any. So when I had an annoyance with another person, it was sort of like the criticism task. Just let go of the criticism. But I added from this task the thought that what was annoying about this other person's behavior was something that I know I've done and continue to do. Then I realized that by choosing to be annoyed by what that person was doing, I was creating distance. And I didn't enjoy the distance, so what was the point? It was helpful to say, "Yeah, I do annoying things, too. I do lots of annoying things."

Bob: I was watching one of those talk shows. Bigots and racists were talking. They were so outrageous!

My blood was boiling about how prejudiced these people were and then I thought of the task. I said, "Lord, forgive me the times when I have been really too much influenced by color or some other thing." I said this quick prayer, "Lord, I'm sorry about my own prejudice."

Session Leader: You see, when you were listening to your "TV bigots," what bothered you was your emotional rage and indignation. You were bothered by your feeling that they were inferior and by your rejection and condemnation of these kids. They were just kids! And putting yourself as the judge over them was non-forgiveness: "I do not forgive you because you are such jerks and bigots."

The attention is all wrong as far as spiritual growth is concerned. Your spiritual growth has nothing to with the people out there. It has to do with you. In shifting the attention and saying,

"Lord, forgive me my prejudices," you're not saying you approve of their prejudices. You're simply saying, "I'm not going to put my energy into making them wrong for being the way they are. Rather, I'm going to acknowledge the times in which I've been in a bad place where I should not have been. I'd rather not be there anymore."

Now, if you were responsible for them, you would have to think very seriously about how you could lead them out of that state. The spiritual task has to do with *your* relationship with your Maker. After you deal with that, then there may be some task you have in relation to other people, but that's another issue altogether. Therefore, it is not for us to go around making accounts of other people: "He owes me this; she owes me that; you owe me this." A failure to forgive becomes a burden on your own spiritual life, and it does not help others.

TASK 12

Handing Your Life over to a Higher Power

I am the vine; you are the branches. Those who remain in me and I in them bear much fruit, because, without me, you are unable to do anything.

John 15:5

John answered and said, "Human beings are unable to receive even one thing unless it has been given to them out of heaven."

John 3:27

I don't know what I'm doing. What I want, I don't do, but what I hate I do.

Romans 7:15

THERE ARE MANY PROGRAMS designed to help people deal with addictions. Some of them have steps beginning with, "We admitted we were powerless. . . ."

People who have struggled with addictions know how true that is. Many of us go through life thinking that we are captains of our own fate, that we have full control over our lives.

The idea that we are, in fact, powerless does not come so easy. This is why we put this task at the end. By the time you have looked at issues like lying, criticizing, living in the present, and forgiving, you will be more open to the thought that you are powerless without help from above.

One morning, I woke up and found that my right arm was almost totally numb. I could not move it. I did not feel anything in my fingers. I reached over with my left hand and picked up my right arm. When I let go, it fell to the mattress as if it were made of wood. Fortunately, it did not take long for the sensations and strength to come back. But the memory stays with me as a vivid reminder that my arm has no power of its own. If it were disconnected from the shoulder, or if the nerves were injured, it would be totally useless. Fortunately, it is connected to something higher, and that gives it power. Its power comes from above.

WHAT POWERS YOU?

A radio receiver can put out a tremendous sound. If you disconnect it from its power source, however, it is totally silent. We can see the electrical plugs that connect various appliances to power sources in our buildings; but we do not see the plugs that connect us with God, and so it seems as if our power comes from ourselves. It seems as if we can think and act for ourselves. We do not realize that thoughts and feelings flow into us from a higher source.

We might attempt to use our own efforts to make changes in our lives. At times, we seem to succeed. At other times, or with other issues, we repeatedly fail. There are some issues that we will never be able to deal with unless we turn to a higher power.

Jesus said that he was the vine and that we are the branches. Any branch that is cut off from the vine withers and dies. We would perish if we were not connected with God.

Life is strange. As children, we learn independence. A child learns to put on her own clothes, or she learns to feed herself. You can hear the pride in a child's voice: "I can do it myself."

But over time, we realize that we are not as much in control of ourselves as we thought and that there are forces in us that we do not understand and cannot manage. Sometimes it takes a crisis, or even a series of crises, for people to come to the point of admitting that they need a higher power in their life. In a way, this is a return to innocence, or a willingness to be led.

In the Bible, this is described as "laying down your life" or "dying." And the wonderful thing is that, when we lay down our life in that way, God gives it back to us. God even gives us a new sense of "heavenly self." This new "self" is a feeling that life *is* our own combined with a total willingness to let God be in charge.

This twelfth task is very personal. That is why we encourage you to create your own task relating to handing your life over to a higher power.

THE TWELFTH TASK

Create a task for yourself relating to handing your life over to the Higher Power. It might take the form of beginning each day with a prayer, such as "God, I give my life to you this day." It could take the form of pausing from time to time to ask, "Lord, what is your will for me at this moment." Find a task that suits where you are in your life at this time.

REPORTING ON THE TASK

Frank: The task I gave myself was to notice when some negative situation or feeling came up, to immediately to hand that situation over to the Lord. I was going through the week; everything was going fine, so I thought, "Oh, maybe I won't get to use the task." Then, today I got a nice big one. It seems trivial when you talk about it, but I think that's characteristic of a lot of these.

I decided it was time to clean up some of the mess in my office and sort through piles of things, and for some reason this is one of the hardest things I have to do in my life. I start going down the pile, and I come to something, and I have no idea what to do with it. I can't throw it away, but there isn't an existing file. I put it in a pile, and pretty soon I find myself distracted, and I haven't gotten anywhere. Negative feelings come up, and I get impatient and annoyed and *phew*. And I could see that's the reason why I never get to the bottom of some piles because too many negative things hit halfway down.

Today I was determined to reduce some of these piles, and I realized the only way I could continue doing it was just to say, "Lord, I'm giving this task to you," and just get centered and work on it for a while. And I get off center, get back, get centered again, work on it for a while. It actually became much more pleasant than it normally would have. I did not get totally through, but I got through a lot of things that I don't think I would have done, so that felt good.

Leslie: I needed to be in a twelve-step program, and I knew this, and I knew that it had been only marginally available to me back home. I would have to drive over an hour each way and into another state just to attend a meeting. That wasn't working for me when I was sick and couldn't travel. In Tucson, there's a meeting that's five minutes from my house, so I went. I went last week and this week, right before this meeting. So I turned this over in a big way. I really feel like I hit bottom somehow with it. There might be farther down to go, but I sure don't want to see what's down there. It's really been difficult.

I thought it was so ironic that I went to this meeting for the first time last week, right before this meeting, and then you gave us the task saying, "Turn something over to your higher power." Okay, done that! My task is finished for the week! I already did it. It's done. It's hard, but it really is a relief, because I, by myself, trying to do this is unmanageable. But I know that with God's help, I can do just fine with it.

Janet: My task was pretty much to let go of control and trust in divine providence and God's will, and let it be. I thought I'd made up my mind about a certain situation, but I'm doing a lot better now that I'm open to all possibilities. The day is better, and I'm just more open and more willing to believe that we all can change. Whatever happens is going to happen, but don't force the issue. Let it evolve.

Stewart: In some of the earlier tasks, I went through sort of a manic period where I was getting up before my two young daughters, and I would do yoga and meditate, and then have a ten-minute prayer session. I was enjoying that so thoroughly. It paved the way for the day in such a wonderful way. And then the last two months or so, it sort of slipped away, and I found myself wanting to sleep in those last few minutes. Then I heard one of the young girls saying, "I'm hungry." So I did that begrudgingly, climbing out of bed rather than springing out of bed with enthusiasm. So my task specifically was to try to get up before the kids and to do some sun salutations, and then to pray.

This week it was actually very tough to do that. I felt as if I'd failed, in that I always heard that little voice. I never beat the kids out of bed. But instead I was able to fit the prayer into the morning ritual with them, and often that was equally rewarding.

This morning, particularly, I was really pretty grumpy and feeling like there's a lot of things to do. I feel like, "Wow, if I worked all morning long, they could make more mess than I could actually clean up." It feels like, "How could that be? How could anyone ever catch up?" So then I try to involve them in the prayer: we sit down and we practice yoga together. They stretch their legs, and they can both get into lotus. My eldest daughter was actually helping: she took her sister away and read her a book while I was doing my meditation, and I was really surprised and pleased this morning. I can take that with me the rest of the day. It tends to make me believe that I'm traveling with the Lord instead of just with my own ego.

Marie: The task that I chose for myself was to be actively loving, because I feel like 98 percent of my life is focused on me, me, me, me. The tasks all helped with that, but I'm convinced . . .

well, there's the positive and the negative, but I always focus on the negative. I've been focusing a lot on "what do I do when a negative feeling comes up?" Instead, this week, I decided to just always try and act lovingly. I mostly wanted to focus on my husband because I feel like he gets the brunt of most of my negativity. I feel safe being mean and jerky to him, whereas I want everybody else to think I'm a nice person. So whenever there was a choice to do a loving thing or to do a selfish thing, I chose this week to do the loving thing.

When I decided about this task, I was really excited. Usually I'm demanding, "I pick the baby-sitter up, and you have to take her home," but this time I was thinking, "I'll take her home if you want." I just felt really happy about that. I don't know if it was easy to do the task because I was in a good mood, or I was in a good mood because I was doing the task, but the whole next day I just felt so happy and free and light.

I think this week I had three times where I felt the happiness of being loving, feeling how wonderful that is, because it's such a pleasure. But so often I choose to be in hell instead of in the heaven of being loving.

Angus: The task I chose was to realize when I was having a situation that was out of control, and then just admit to God that this is way beyond my control. I decided to invite him to help me out with it. It really made me realize how many situations I have and how many things I have going on that are just beyond my control. I think it's sort of ego to think you are able to fix everything in your life and handle it, but it's really gotten to the point where I can't. I realized that a lot this week. I didn't really end up feeling any better about it, but it did make me realize that I have been offered a lot of help that I chose not to accept, just because I was really choosing to try to deal with it on my own.

I started thinking, "That's really ungracious." Like a lot of times, if I play a gig or something, people will come up afterward and give me a compliment. They'll say, "That was really good," and I'll go, "Yeah, thanks, but I screwed up that other part." Someone pointed out to me once that that was really a rude thing to do. When someone wants to do something nice for you, like give you a compliment, it makes them feel good to do it, and then when you turn it around and refuse it, then it makes them feel bad.

So I thought that I've been refusing all this help, and I thought that really wasn't very nice. But it's where I was at the time. I just felt like, fifty times a day, it would happen to me, and I would just invite God and say, "I need a lot of help with this." So I think I'm going to take up some of the offers of help I've had.

Darren: My task this week coincided with another task from a twelve-step group, the ninth step of apologizing. But it involved really trying to hand over my apologies to God, so that I was being a vessel of God in the apology and not allowing it to be a self-serving apology, in the sense of having the intention being, "I want this person to like me again, or think well of me," and really have it be for them. The interesting thing was I did notice that I was aware of the Lord, and tried to have it really be for that person.

Nicole: Last week I was feeling really overwhelmed with stuff for school and the end of the semester. Then I started thinking, "What am I going to do after?" I have the next semester planned, and then I don't know what I'm going to do after that. I'm just kind of letting myself get into this: "What am I doing this for? What am I going to do after I go to school?" I was worried about some relationship stuff too. And when we talked about what we were going to do for the task, I think that was the biggest part of the week for me, just reminding myself that everything is happening the way it's supposed to be. Sometimes I'm really good at remembering that, and sometimes I'm not at all. I'll start getting into this downward spiral of worrying about things. But then sometimes, you know, things hadn't changed since the day before, I still don't know what I'm doing, but I feel fine with it. So just reminding myself—just having this task come up—that was about handing it over to God. So I pretty much just decided for myself that when I was feeling overwhelmed, that I just prayed and remember that everything is going the way it's supposed to, and God has a plan for me. Actually, it was a pretty good week after our meeting.

Keri: My task is to ask God what his will for me is at this moment. I was just going to do it periodically. Tuesday morning, my alarm went off, and I pressed "snooze," and it went off again, and I pressed "snooze," and then I got up and kneeled down and started to pray, and I asked God what his will is for me, and I swear he told me to press "snooze." I thought that was pretty cool. It's like, "Okay, you're okay, you're on my side." It kind of set the tone for the rest of the week. I think I might have needed some extra sleep.

I had a couple of times where I asked God what his will was for me, and I felt like he answered me in different ways. One time I was having trouble making a decision, and there was someone waiting for me to make the decision. I kind of knew what I wanted, but I didn't know how to say what I wanted without feeling like I was going to hurt that person's feelings. I didn't feel like it was a personal thing. It was my choice, about wanting to be by myself. And he just told me how I could do it. He just said, "Why don't you just walk the person out to the car, and be cheerful, and that'll be a really nice time." And I hadn't thought of any of that; I was just thinking, "Oh, they're going to have hurt feelings." But then he just told me how to do it. And I was like, "Oh, good. I can have what I want, and not make someone else sad." Another time I asked, and I felt like it was kind of an important decision and I really didn't know what I wanted. I felt like he said, "It's up to you. Either way works, so just do what you want." And that felt really nice, because I thought I was going to have to do one thing. I thought that one was probably the right thing, and the other was probably the wrong thing, but I felt like he said, "You can do whatever you want here." I was like, "Cool. All right!"

Then I asked him a couple of times, even though there wasn't any decision pending. I was just like, "God, I want to know what your will is for me." Hoping that he would show me how to feel, or what to think. And I think he did, but I don't really remember. But it was a good feeling, a nice safe feeling to feel like it wasn't all up to me, because I don't really enjoy that much responsibility.

Elly: My task was just chilling out, and letting God take care of my life. It seemed like kind of a silly task, and I kind of wanted to change it afterward. I was thinking, "No, there is a reason why I chose it." So I just stayed with it all week. I prayed a lot more than normal, because it was a challenging week, with lots of spiritual opportunities for growth.

The task was very beneficial. Lots of the time, I think about the quality of my life and what I want for my own life. For so long, being a minister's daughter, I had built up this whole wall of rejection and rebelliousness against organized religion and God in general. Or God in specific. And that wall's crumbling down a little bit, and that feels good, that I can just have my own relationship, independent of family ties or expectations or that kind of thing. I realized, especially this week, because it was challenging, that my quality of life is infinitely so much better when God's in it.

Noomay: I was really touched by the guided meditation where one of us was talking about the Lord holding us. I wanted to really feel the Lord holding me. I thought about how hard it was for me to do. And then thinking back on times in my life when I do let the Lord hold me, just how tender it is. So I decided that's what I wanted to try to do every day, just for a moment—to try to feel the Lord holding me.

The first night it was great, because I was really on top and focused. I lit candles, and it was so fun to let go, and sing to the Lord. I felt like I could do anything, and yet it wasn't me doing anything; it was me *not* doing anything, letting the Lord be there. So that was probably the most fun day.

Throughout the week, each day was a little different, but I did remember the task every day, which is shocking to me because I'm pretty inconsistent with a lot of things. One night I had gone to sleep, and I woke up—I don't know why I woke up—but "Oh no, I didn't do the task!" And so it gave me a chance to focus and feel like, "Wow, I wasn't aware of the Lord, and I couldn't have done the task that day because I can't do anything without the Lord." It was fun to have awareness, and see how far I really need to go in terms of letting the Lord take over my life.

Klara: I was going to try to focus on what I feel is the source of some pain for me. It has a lot to do with forgiving a specific person, that I've been working on for a long time. Not getting very far. So I did a lot of praying; that was the avenue that I chose. Just pray a lot about it, and I also used the forgiveness task a lot, and I found really helpful the idea of canceling a debt. I also really tried to think of, "What might some other people feel like I owe them? What are my debts? What are some actual debts that I can acknowledge, and what are some possible debts that others may feel?" That was helpful too, to see that well, there could be some people out there feeling like I owe them. It was helpful to think of it in those terms instead of, like, this specific horrible person. And I just sort of looked at it outside myself a little bit more.

Greg: The task that I've taken on is basically to do a little better job about managing stress. Looking at the beginning of this year that's about to begin, I realize I'd just taken on an awful lot. What I want to try to do is to work on those tasks and things that I've committed myself to do in a way that I don't lose the spirit of generosity and helpfulness that made me volunteer to do them in the first place.

I find it's easy to get overextended, and then once I've done that, to start feeling very, very stressed, and then it all turns on itself. And instead of something that's a cheerfully undertaken task that you're doing for others, you begin to feel yourself a martyr and then feel resentful about these things that you cheerfully began. I realize it was maybe going to take more than just a general awareness that the risk was there, that I was going to have some kind of disciplines or tools to get in front of all that so that it wouldn't occur. And so the task I've set myself is to really do more conscious meditation and praying, so that I can have a little bit of distance from the almost inevitable stress that's going to come.

Bob: Long ago, when I first worked this program, a lady named Betsy Gladdish provided the most beautiful and moving report on this task. I would like to share it with you just as she reported: "I did the task as an invitation:

Dear Lord, You are invited to a person-warming (instead of a house warming) The day is today and forever. The place is in my mind, body, and spirit. I am inviting you to dwell inside my mind so that my thoughts are positive, loving and productive.

I ask you to live within my body so that I am healthy, energetic, and able to serve your world. I ask you to abide in my spirit so that I may do your will every day, seeing my life through your eyes.

Please come with work for me to do, and love for me to give. In return, I will greet you each morning as I look into the mirror, and ask your will for me today. I will meet you for breakfast, lunch, and dinner with a prayer of thanksgiving. I will walk with you in the morning, and know you sing to me with your birds, and smile on me with your sunshine. Throughout the day, I will acknowledge your presence in any good I might do or receive, and I will close the day full of gratitude for your love and a deep faith in your presence. You have always been at my door.

Welcome, welcome. I love you."

THE VALUE OF SPIRITUAL GROWTH

As we have pointed out on many occasions, spiritual growth can take as many paths as there are people willing to set out on the journey. Many participants in this series of spiritual growth tasks have expressed the meaning of this program to them personally.

Here are some thoughts of those people with whom you have shared the journey on the road to spiritual growth. By now you probably feel that each of them is a new friend who has shared some of his or her life experiences with you.

Keri: I felt like we were a team, and that was cool for me. I don't always have the easiest time feeling comfortable being close to people, but I felt like this was a very comfortable group. It felt like a breakthrough for me, in terms of sharing with people and believing that people care about me and recognizing that I care about them. That may all sound really fundamental, but sometimes it takes a while. So I feel really happy and grateful.

Nicole: I've been thinking about how it's been good to have people for support. If I'm in a negative place, and have other people remind me about the task or a different task that we worked a couple of weeks ago that helps me. I really like having something concrete to work on. I have one specific thing each week to really think about. That's helpful for me.

Being conscious of the fact that there are tools gives me something active to do, instead of just dwelling in the negative space for a long time. It still comes up, but it doesn't last as long. I just feel like you can do something about it instead of sulking, so I really appreciate that.

Leslie: I really appreciate having something that I'm working on, and then coming in and getting a chance to hear what happened for other people when they tried to work on the same thing. It gives me a chance to feel more connected to people and less isolated. When I try to do a task like this, I usually am prone to thinking that I'm a real failure, I haven't executed it perfectly, so it's helpful to listen to other people's processes and get insights that way. I've gotten a lot of insights from this group that I've applied in my life.

Angus: I was just thinking that the first time I walked into the group I had really no idea what to expect. I was nervous, because I hadn't really been involved with church or God or anything for a long time, and wasn't sure I was ready to get that going again. But it didn't take very long to get into it. I can really say I haven't met a nicer group of people. I like everybody in this room. Everybody is nice. I guess it's rare, I don't know. But it seems like everybody has something in common, because they're interested in doing spiritual work.

I definitely feel like now I have some tools to work with. I really felt like, before this program, I was trying hard to change things and make things better, but it wasn't quite working for me. I feel like this group has profoundly changed my life, on many levels, and now I feel like I understand why things weren't working because I was approaching them from the wrong direction. This experience has changed my life, through the people that I've met and the things that I've learned. It's been great.

Darren: I definitely noticed that living in line with my beliefs isn't so easy. But group support makes a huge difference, especially being in a group where everyone's working the same task, whether it be a twelve-step with the same addiction or in this spiritual growth. The fact that we're all in here working together definitely makes me feel like part of a team. I don't feel like I'm alone; even when I'm without this group and something comes up, I don't feel I'm the only one working this. I feel like the group is there with me, supporting me and helping me. And I just thought the thing I had to offer the group would be what I would say, and I'm just getting to know that the best thing I could offer is listening.

What I love most about these tasks is that they focus on in the negativity within, but for very positive and productive reasons. So instead of being hard on myself and thinking, "Man, I'm terrible! I don't listen to anybody!" I think, "Wow, what an opportunity. The next time I'm in a group, I'll let listening be a huge, ambitious task." So it's neat to be able to feel positive about it, instead of negative.

Janet: I'm going to miss this group. It was news to me that this was our last meeting. It was like, "Oh no! What will I do?" I depended on you all being here. This is the second time I've been through these twelve steps. The first time was a different group and they were nice people, but I just feel a synergy. You all are younger, but seem to be, I don't know, more advanced spiritually. Maybe it's just the way the group interacts, or maybe it's me in a different stage in my life and how I perceive it. It's been a joy to get to know the new people that I didn't know before. And I'll miss you.

Noomay: I really enjoyed this group. It was fun. I learned a lot. I feel like I'll never graduate from these twelve tasks. But it feels really good and feels really exciting. I love the group. I'm a lazy, procrastinating kind of person, so it's really needed for me to be able to come every week. It'll be hard not to know what to do. When does the next one start?

Marie: I feel like I was able to listen to everybody, and I feel so much more connected. And also, letting go of control of my own sharing, like it's okay if I ramble on and on, and it's okay if I don't say things perfectly. So that I just let things come, and let blank spots come.

I think the thing I like the best about the spiritual-growth group is just seeing tragedy and negativity and bad things that happen in my life as opportunities. Before it was like, "Oh no, why is this happening to me?" But now it's like, "Oh, look, I get an opportunity to work on my spiritual growth. Thank you." And being grateful for that, because I really feel like it is an opportunity and I don't just say that. I kind of get excited, like, "Oh, now what tools can I use today?"

Elly: My closing thoughts have already been said, so I will just say that I'm very grateful to everybody. I think we had really good group dynamics. I remember telling someone why we are in the course, and I said something like, "Because this is like spiritual vitamins." And that still holds true. I'm amazed what a staple in my week this has become. When I had to miss it for two weeks, it really upset me.

I feel as much as sometimes I like to share, I really like the listening part. I feel even if I never said a word, I could sit here and listen to everyone else and still go home and feel like, "Wow, I'm ready to start tomorrow, and I feel really inspired." I always go home, and I feel a little bit elated, a little bit better about life in general.

Greg: This has been a remarkable experience for me. One of the best things about it is I think the program has made us all a lot more forthcoming in seeing this is a safe place where we could say things. But aside from that, I think the practices that are built into each week's lessons are the valuable part. You're striving for a state or for a place, and it's hard to know how to get there without some real tools. I think one of the things that's been most valuable for me is using the task sheets and the quotes and passages that are there as vehicles, really understanding that there's that connection between practice, discipline, and then a state that you're trying to arrive at. Maybe you don't quite get there, but you have these practices that set you on the road. And I think having that kind of structure has just been a really wonderful thing and a remarkably effective tool.

Klara: I'm really going to miss coming here when we go back to Seattle. I'm just going to miss everybody. It's been a great experience. I can remember at some point during the course feeling like, "Wow, I don't have any hope of reaching my goal. I'm just really disappointed, I haven't been any good," I'm feeling a lot better now at the end. I feel like the tasks were really helpful and had a cumulative effect. I'm going to be taking that back with me and using them. Again, I find that I do automatically use the ones that come to mind as the appropriate task. Some of the ones that I really enjoy I'm just going to do because I enjoyed them.

Bob: Spiritual growth has become a way of life for me. I think it is a way of practicing my religion on a day-to-day basis. I'm grateful for the insights it has provided me in my life's journey. The road is never easy to travel, but each day I see a small glimpse of heaven in the peace of mind that I have achieved through my spiritual work.

Session Leader: There's really been something very, very special about this group, and so I feel very honored that this group allowed itself to be taped because I think this is one for the books.

BRINGING IT ALL TOGETHER

A T THIS POINT, most readers have recognized the pattern of our twelve tasks. They begin by exploring the levels of life in our relationship with ourselves. We then work together on our relationship with others and examine the impact of others on our spiritual well-being. Finally, we work on our relationship with our God.

In this concluding chapter, let us review the series of goals in relationship to the tasks we have worked together.

SPIRITUAL GROWTH TASKS

WAKING UP TO SPIRITUAL LIFE

1. When you notice a negative emotion, divide your attention. Focus part of your attention on the back of your hand.

We are waking up to spiritual life and discovering that we have higher levels in ourselves.

Lesson Objective: To demonstrate that we can choose to focus on positive and higher levels when negatives invade our consciousness.

DEALING WITH DIFFICULT EMOTIONS

2. When you are conscious of a negative emotion, experiment with stopping the negative thought. Observe the negative thoughts that come with the emotion.

We are learning about the emotion-thought connection, how to eliminate negative feelings by stopping negative thoughts.

Lesson Objective: To demonstrate that we can break the connection between negative thought and negative emotion by interjecting a positive thought.

IDENTIFYING WITH POSITIVE EMOTIONS

3. When you become aware of a negative emotion in yourself, say, "*It* is, but I don't have to be."

We are learning to separate ourselves from our negative emotions and not identify with them.

Lesson Objective: To demonstrate that the emotion we are experiencing at a given moment is not the sum total of our being and that we can consciously separate ourselves from the negative emotion.

LETTING GO OF CRITICISM

4. Observe your criticisms; then go for a whole day without internal or external criticisms.

We are letting go of criticisms of ourselves and of others.

Lesson Objective: To demonstrate that we can thwart the tendency to drag ourselves down by criticism of others and ourselves.

APPLYING THE GOLDEN RULE

5. When you have negative thoughts about another person, put yourself in his or her shoes. Find one positive and true thought about that person.

We are replacing negative thoughts about others with positive ones.

Lesson Objective: To demonstrate that a negative viewpoint of another can be replaced by a positive one by forcing positive thoughts about that person into our conscious thoughts.

TAMING THE WILD ELEPHANT

6. When a negative emotion is active in you, become aware of your body tensions. Relax your body and replace negative thoughts with positive ones.

We are learning how to "tame the wild elephant" by relaxing the body and using positive thoughts.

Lesson Objective: To demonstrate that body tension drives negative thought and emotion, and that relaxation of mind and body can reduce the impact of those negatives.

DEALING WITH LYING

7. Observe yourself lying. Stop the lying as soon as you notice.

We are observing and stopping forms of lying.

Lesson Objective: To demonstrate that love of truth is necessary to our spiritual well-being and that recognizing our lies and stopping the lying will elevate us to higher levels of spiritual well-being.

LIVING IN THE PRESENT

8. When you feel regret or anxiety, observe any connection with the past or future. Let go and bring yourself into an awareness of something positive in the here and now.

We are learning to live in the present.

Lesson Objective: To demonstrate that the present moment is the crux of our spiritual existence and that worry about the future or regret about the past can destroy spiritual life.

DEALING WITH FALSE CAUSE

9. Whenever you feel upset, stop and remember that upsets do not come from outside you, but from inside. Observe your reactions from that point of view.

We are learning not to be deceived by false cause and discovering that all causes are spiritual.

Lesson Objective: To recognize that most causes of negative emotion and negative thought are lies and based on falsities.

CHOOSING HIGHER DELIGHTS

10. When you suspect that you are in a negative state, notice enjoyment you may be having from it. Let go of the negative and see if you can allow the positive to take its place.

We are discovering levels of delight and deciding to choose higher delights over lower ones.

Lesson Objective: To demonstrate that we can choose a new attitude, new pursuits, or endeavors that enable us to enjoy life on a deeper level

FORGIVING OTHERS

11. When a person trespasses against you, use effort and attention to recall something you would ask the Lord to forgive you for. Hold them side by side.

We are learning to forgive others and ourselves.

Lesson Objective: To demonstrate that we can view a transgression from a spiritual viewpoint and that we can visualize transgressions for which we need forgiveness, thus redirecting our emotions to a positive momentum.

HANDING YOUR LIFE OVER TO A HIGHER POWER

12. Hand your life over to a higher power. Begin each day with a prayer, and pause to ask God's will in your life.

We are handing our life over to whatever God we recognize.

Lesson Objective: To admit that we have very limited power in the events that shape our lives and that our destiny is shaped by our ability to let our higher power's will become a conscious and integral part of our daily existence.

These twelve tasks are just the beginning. The pattern described above can be repeated endlessly, taking on new form and new meaning with each iteration. The theme remains the same: gain an ongoing and closer relationship with your God by removing those obstacles that block out the flow of love into your life.

CLOSING SESSIONS

At Sunrise Chapel in Tucson, Arizona, where the spiritual-growth movement has been fostered and nurtured, we often use a meditation to begin a session of sharing. Here is a relaxation technique, followed by a meditation. We believe that our meditations express the peace of mind that you achieve by regularly working on growing closer to your God.

Relaxation Technique

Close your eyes and start to relax. Become aware of your body. Notice any centers of tension that you need to let go of to be comfortable.

Soon you start breathing evenly and gently, in and out. With each inward breath, bring in the life-giving oxygen to fill your lungs, to be carried through your blood to every cell in your body, renewing and revitalizing. This life-giving oxygen feeds your whole body and brings newness and freshness into your life.

And as you breathe out, let go of any negativity, any staleness, anything that you would like to get rid of. Just breathe it out with your breath and it will be gone. As you continue to breathe gently and evenly, feel your muscles go loose and limp. You find your body getting heavier and heavier and more relaxed. Just let go and enjoy that wonderful feeling of relaxation—the oxygen coming into your body and staleness and negativity going out. Now notice any thoughts that are floating in your mind. Give them a moment of attention and then let go. If they are important, they will come back when you need them. If they're not, let them float away, and soon you have the feeling that your mind is clear and clean. You begin to feel a mental relaxation to match the physical relaxation in your body.

Let go of any thoughts that are hovering around. Right now your mind can relax completely. Right now you don't need any of those thoughts. Right now you can let your mind be clean, clear, and ready to receive whatever comes to it. Each time you breathe out, relax.

You begin to approach a deeper part of your being that is always at peace, that is always in touch with your higher self, the part of you in harmony with the whole universe, a peaceful, restful place. This is your retreat where you can come whenever you need it. It is always there for you. This higher level of your being dwells in perfect harmony, looks down on your daily life, and passes along its blessings of peace.

A Meditation

All the different parts of God's grand and glorious creation fit together to form a complete and beautiful whole. I am a unique part of God's creation with my own role to fill and my own special gifts to give. The people around me need the gifts I have to give, and more importantly I need to give what is mine to give.

As I open my mind and heart to God, I receive new clarity and insight. I see myself as God created me, gifted and talented and needed beyond the furthest stretch of my imagination, welcomed and at one with life wherever I am.

Wherever I go, my personality is the way that I present myself to the world. My body is the vehicle through which my spirit lives and expresses itself. My mind is an instrument for the expression of divine ideas, for I am an eternal spiritual being. My true higher self is undisturbed by outer conditions and circumstances. I remind myself again that I am a spiritual being. I remember that God is my sure and certain guide through all experiences. I know that God is in charge, and I am willing to work with God's plan for good. I am able to express love easily. I know that I am a coworker with God. As a spiritual being, I am expressing God's likeness.

I know that I am a spiritual being, created in the image and likeness of God. On the deepest level, I am at peace and in harmony with the universe. I have a body, but I am not my body. I have feelings, but I am not my feelings. I have thoughts, but I am not my thoughts. I am a beloved child of God, a vessel. He works through me as his instrument. I find my greatest fulfillment when his love passes through me to others who are also his children, who are also created in his image and likeness.

As his love passes through me, I remove those barriers that would stand in its way so that it can flow freely through me to others. I long to remove anything in myself that would impede the flow. I know that I am privileged to be part of the grand plan whereby I can pass on these gifts to others. I feel grateful to be allowed to participate in this great work.

As I place my life in God's hands, I know that I am safe, that nothing can harm me, that his loving arms will embrace me and protect me wherever I go.

Thank you, Lord, for loving me.

The Lord's Prayer

We often close our sessions with this unique translation by Jonathan Rose of the Lord's Prayer.

> Our Father in heaven, your name must be kept holy. Your kingdom must come. Your will must be done on earth as in heaven. Give us day by day our daily bread. And forgive us our sins, for we also forgive everyone who is indebted to us. And do not lead us into a trial, but deliver us from the evil one. Amen.

Finally, closing sessions with recorded music as a background for silent prayer or meditation can also be an effective method to help participants become centered and reflect on their spiritual growth.

The material in this book is based on seminars presented at the Sunrise Chapel in Tucson, Arizona. Additional materials, including recorded lessons, leader notes, recorded meditations, and illustrated handouts for sixty additional tasks are available from the Arizona Spiritual Growth Foundation.

THE GROUP

Angus has a B.A. in music and is unmarried. He is currently recording his first CD, which is scheduled for release in the fall of 1999.

Bob is coauthor of this book. See "About the Authors."

Darren owns a yoga studio and is a yoga instructor. He is married.

Elly is a freelance writer and editor, who loves travel, stained glass, and international politics. She has a B.S. in journalism and political science. She feels that participating in the spiritual-growth group was the best decision she has ever made.

Frank is coauthor of this book. See "About the Authors."

Greg is a law professor. He is married to Klara, and they have an infant son. Greg is also the father of a ten-year-old boy. He is active in community service, especially the arts and environmental affairs. He enjoys fly-fishing and recently began studying the cello.

Janet is a married student, who has returned to university study after working as a respiratory therapist for a number of years.

Keri has a B.A. in English and is single. For the past two years, she has worked at a law firm, but is now studying Shiatsu, a kind of massage. Keri took the Spiritual Growth seminar to experience people on a more authentic level and to become a better person.

Klara recently celebrated her first wedding anniversary with Greg and welcomed their son Christopher Henry into the world. She received a degree in law from the University of Washington Law School in 1996 and currently works part-time from her home in the area of securities law.

Leslie holds advanced degrees and has a professional career. She is also an artist, musician, and herbalist. She is unmarried.

Marie has been married for eight years and has two young daughters. She has a Master's in Special Education and teaches part-time in a bilingual public school. Her goal in joining this seminar was to bring more joy and peace into her life.

Nicole has a degree in education, and she is currently studying art. She is unmarried.

Noomay is a young woman in her early twenties. She is engaged to married. After three years of college, she is taking a break and working at a variety of jobs. Noomay felt she needed specific tools to help her live her life with as much awareness as possible.

Stewart is married and the father of two children. He holds a B.A. and works in graphic design. He joined the seminar to gain tools for dealing with all the negative energy in his life and to find joy.

SUGGESTED READINGS

Alcoholics Anonymous: The Big Book. New York: AA World Services, Inc., 1995.

Bradshaw, John. *Creating Love: The Next Great Stage of Growth.* New York: Bantam, 1992.

Burns, David. *Feeling Good: The New Mood Therapy.* New York: William Morrow & Company, 1980.

Cameron, Julia. *The Artist's Way.* New York: Tarcher, 1992.

Carlson, Richard. *Don't Sweat the Small Stuff—And It's All Small Stuff.* New York: Hyperion, 1997.

————. *Don't Sweat the Small Stuff with Your Family: Simple Ways to Keep Daily Responsibilities and Household Chaos from Taking over Your Life.* New York: Hyperion: 1998.

Carlson, Richard, and Wayne W. Dyer. *You Can Be Happy No Matter What: Five Principles for Keeping Life in Perspective.* New York: New World Library, 1997.

Carlson, Richard; Benjamin Shield; and Marianne Williamson, eds. *For the Love of God: Handbook for the Spirit.* New York: New World Library: 1997.

————. *Handbook for the Soul.* Boston: Little, Brown and Co., 1995.

Chopra, Deepak. *The Seven Spiritual Laws of Success.* San Rafael, CA: Amber-Allen Publishing, 1994.

————. *Unconditional Life.* New York: Bantam, 1991.

————. *The Path to Love and Quantum Healing.* New York: Bantam, 1991.

Dole, George. *A Thoughtful Soul: Reflections from Swedenborg.* West Chester, Penna.: Chrysalis Books, 1995.

Dyer, Wayne W. *Manifest Your Destiny.* New York: Harper Perennial, 1997.

———. *Your Erroneous Zones.* New York: Avon, 1976.

Gerzon, Robert. *Finding Serenity in the Age of Anxieties.* New York: MacMillan, 1997.

Goleman, Daniel. *Emotional Intelligence.* New York: Bantam Books, 1995.

Grof, Stanislaf. *The Adventure of Self-Discovery.* New York: State University of New York Press, 1988.

Howard, Alice, and Walden Howard. *Exploring the Road Less Traveled.* New York: Simon and Schuster, 1985.

Jampolsky, Gerald G. *Love is Letting Go of Fear.* Berkeley, Calif.: Celestial Arts, 1979.

Kline, Thomas L. *The Journey of Life.* Bryn Athyn, Penna.: General Church Press, 1989.

LeShaw, Larry. *How to Meditate: A Tape.* Los Angeles: Los Angeles Audio Renaissance, 1987.

McGraw, Phillip C. *Life Strategies.* New York: Hyperion, 1999.

Nicoll, Maurice. *Psychological Commentaries on the Teachings of Gurdjieff and Ouspensky.* 5 volumes. Boston: Shambhala, 1984, 1985.

Peck, M. Scott. *Further Along the Road Less Traveled.* New York: Simon and Schuster, 1985.

Prager, Dennis. *Happiness is a Serious Problem.* New York: Regan Books, Harper Collins, 1996.

Rhodes, Peter S. *Aim: The Workbook.* San Francisco: Johnny Appleseed and Co., 1994.

———. "Aim." Unpublished manuscript, 1991.

Schnarr, Grant R. *Return to the Promised Land.* West Chester, Penna.: Chrysalis Books, 1997

———. *Spiritual Recovery: A Twelve-Step Guide.* West Chester, Penna.: Chrysalis Books, 1998.

Swedenborg, Emanuel, *Arcana Coelestia.* 12 volumes. Trans. John F. Potts. Second edition. West Chester, Penna.: Swedenborg Foundation, 1995–1998.

————. *Apocalypse Revealed.* 2 volumes. Trans. John Whitehead. Second edition. West Chester, Penna.: Swedenborg Foundation, 1997.

————. *Divine Love and Wisdom.* Trans. John C. Ager. Second edition. West Chester, Penna.: Swedenborg Foundation, 1995.

————. *Divine Providence.* Trans. William Wunsch. Second edition. West Chester, Penna.: Swedenborg Foundation, 1995.

————. *True Christian Religion.* 2 volumes. Trans. John C. Ager. Second edition. West Chester, Penna.: Swedenborg Foundation, 1996.

Taylor, Eugene. *A Psychology of Spiritual Healing.* West Chester, Penna.: Chrysalis Books, 1997.

Van Dusen, Wilson. *The Natural Depth in Man.* West Chester, Penna.: Swedenborg Foundation, 1990.

ABOUT THE AUTHORS

Frank Rose received a Master of Divinity from the Academy of the New Church in Bryn Athyn, Pennsylvania, where he also taught. He has served as pastor to groups in England, Scotland, Wales, Holland, Belgium, France, and Canada.

Frank and his wife Louise currently live in Tucson, Arizona, where, in 1982, Frank became pastor of the Sunrise Chapel congregation. Noticing a need for applying Christianity, the Roses and a group of others began the Spiritual Growth Program in 1988. Frank is a founder and chairman of the board of the Arizona Spiritual Growth Foundation, Inc.

Robert Maginel was born in a small North Dakota town and traveled extensively in his youth. Bob is now a retired Air Force colonel who served in command and headquarters assignments for over twenty-two years. He has lived throughout the United States as well as in Europe and Asia.

Bob holds a BBA in management from the University of Texas and a Masters of Science from the Air Force Institute of Technology. On retirement from the Air Force, he founded Mobility Manufacturing, Incorporated, and served as chairman and CEO until 1994. He has led many spiritual-growth groups in the past several years and is a founder of the Arizona Spiritual Growth Foundation, Inc. He currently serves as CEO and board member for the foundation.

SPIRITUAL RECOVERY
A TWELVE-STEP GUIDE
Grant Schnarr

"...Schnarr listens to the heart and discounts irrelevant dogmas."
—*Publishers Weekly*

Using a twelve-step approach, Grant Schnarr presents a path to freedom, away from destructive tendencies, toward greater awareness of others, self, and God. Filled with practical advice for incorporating the twelve steps into life, *Spiritual Recovery* also explains why each step works.

0-87785-379-7, pb, $13.95

RETURN TO THE PROMISED LAND: THE STORY OF OUR SPIRITUAL RECOVERY
Grant Schnarr

"Schnarr...enable[s] those seeking spiritual recovery to move from the fury of inner spiritual warfare, to lasting peace." —*Publishers Weekly*

Return to the Promised Land is a guide for spiritual recovery that draws upon the biblical symbolism of the Exodus story. Schnarr compares the Israelites' struggles in the wilderness to our own life crises. Practical, twelve-step exercises help the reader escape the ego's tyranny, and hold on to hope in stressful times.

0-87785-179-4 pb, $12.95

LIGHT IN MY DARKNESS
Helen Keller; Edited by Ray Silverman

"...an inspiring picture of this remarkable woman's aY rmation of the power and triumph of the spirit."
—*New Age Retailer*

Helen Keller's optimism and service to humanity were inspired by her readings of Swedenborg, whose insights she called her "strongest incitement to overcome limitations." This is Keller's 1927 spiritual autobiography, revised and enlarged with her letters, speeches, and other writings.

0-87785-146-8, pb, photos, $12.95

ANGELS IN ACTION
WHAT SWEDENBORG SAW AND HEARD
Robert H. Kirven

"Kirven presents Swedenborg's ideas and defends and promotes them in modern terms." —*Booklist*

For the last twenty-seven years of his life, Emanuel Swedenborg visited heaven and hell almost daily, meeting angels and evil spirits. His visions and their meanings are explained in this remarkable book. Kirven shows how angels work for us from birth through death and how we can be angels on earth.

0-87785-147-6, pb, illus., $11.95

A SCIENTIST EXPLORES SPIRIT
A BIOGRAPHY OF EMANUEL SWEDENBORG, WITH KEY CONCEPTS OF HIS THEOLOGY
George F. Dole and Robert H. Kirven

"Swedenborg is like a whole Himalayan Range of the mind. This biography, ...as from a mountain top, presents the whole vista of wisdom."
—*Wilson Van Dusen*

This lively, concise revision introduces the life and spiritual thought of Emanuel Swedenborg. Of interest is the tension between science and spirit, and their ultimate conXuence in Swedenborg,s life and work.

0-87785-241-3, pb, illus., $10.95

HIDDEN MILLENNIUM
THE DOOMSDAY FALLACY
Stephen Koke
Foreword by David Spangler

"A balanced, concise, well-documented account of speculation and concern about the millennium.... Quite an absorbing book." —*Booklist*

Summarizing traditional millennial movements, *Hidden Millennium* explains why past doomsday prophesies have failed to materialize. Dire predictions contrast with the symbolic interpretation oVered by Emanuel Swedenborg, who sees the Last Judgment as personal, not worldly, and hopeful, not fearful.

0-87785-376-2, pb, $14.95

DECISIONS! DECISIONS!
THE DYNAMICS OF CHOICE
Carol S. Lawson
& Robert F. Lawson, Editors
Foreword by Susan Cheever

This illustrated collection of original stories, poems, and essays broadens and brightens our pathways of possibilities. The richness and clarity of reXection show that the care taken to understand the context and the intent of decision are as important as the "yea" or "nay" of the choice itself.

0-87785-230-8, pb, 160 pp, illus., $13.95,
SIXTH CHRYSALIS READER

HEAVEN & HELL
Emanuel Swedenborg
Translated by George F. Dole

"One of the most fascinating guides to other worlds in the Western spiritual canon." —Gary Lachman, *Gnosis*

First published in 1758, *Heaven and Hell* fully describes the life hereafter. Dole's easy-to-read translation makes Swedenborg's experiences accessible to all. Swedenborg describes heaven, the world of spirits, and hell, and explains their meaning and relationship to our lives in the earthly realm.

0-87785-153-0, pb, $12.95

VIDEOTAPES

SWEDENBORG:\
THE MAN WHO HAD TO KNOW
with Lillian Gish; Eddie Albert, narrator.

Televised over 2,500 times, this Wlm presents one of history's most fascinating personalities, Emanuel Swedenborg, and depicts his visionary insights.

VHS, 30 min, $29.95

JOHNNY APPLESEED
AND THE FRONTIER WITHIN
with Lillian Gish

The true story of American folk hero Johnny "Appleseed" Chapman, frontier mystic and self-appointed Swedenborgian minister. Cross the ultimate threshold.

VHS, 30 min, $29.95

Available at bookstores, or:

Individuals:
Call **800-355-3222**
or order through our secured web site at **www.swedenborg.com**

or write:
Swedenborg Foundation Publishers
320 North Church Street
West Chester, PA 19380

Booksellers: (for books only)
Call Words Distributing Company
800-593-WORD (9673)